FINDING
GOD
IN CHAOS

D0880306

MIKE DENIGAN

Finding God in Chaos

Copyright © 2020 by Mike Denigan

Published by Free the Nations

ISBN: 978-0-9600539-3-3

Dedication

This book is dedicated to my family. It is difficult to pursue the call of God effectively without having a supportive family. I am grateful for my wife, Robin, and our three children: Trey, Summer, and Brice. They have made many sacrifices so that others can be set free.

To my parents, Michael and Ella Denigan, my biggest fans: Thanks for all your unwavering and unshakable love and support. To my in-laws, Malcolm and Mary Pugh: I am forever grateful for your grace, love, and many prayers.

You are all greatly loved and appreciated.

Endorsement

Nothing is more becoming than a man of God on fire with passion. A question for every believer is never can we trust God; the question is can God trust us?

As you read this book, you will realize Mike Denigan is a man with an entrustment from God for this generation. The powerful stories of deliverance will cause you to take heart, for God will never leave Himself without a witness.

I have known the author from his childhood and can vouch for his character and integrity as a dedicated follower of Jesus of Nazareth.

– Pastor Cleddie Keith

Contents

Foreword 9

Introduction 11

Chapter 1: Seek First 13

Chapter 2: The Melody of the Holy Ghost 19

Chapter 3: Heaven's Army 25

Chapter 4: Jesus! Help Me! 31

Chapter 5: The Miracle Patient 37

Chapter 6: Keep Praying 43

Chapter 7: God's in the Crazy 49

Chapter 8: The Kneeling Jihadist 53

Chapter 9: Going to the Other Side 59

Chapter 10: As Petty as an Airline Seat 67

Chapter 11: A Sign for a Housekeeper 71

Chapter 12: Darkness Defeated 77

Chapter 13: Catalyst 83

Chapter 14: Master Class 89

Chapter 15: Don't Worry. Jesus is with Us 95

Chapter 16: Troubles in this World 101

Chapter 17: The Midnight Hour 107

Chapter 18: Fire Beetle Christians 113

Chapter 19: Stepping into Another's Chaos 119

Chapter 20: Inconvenient Surrender 125

Chapter 21: Stand Your Ground 131

Chapter 22: Finding God in Ziklag 139

The Final Chapter 143

Foreword

I thank God for this fiery minister of God, Mike Denigan, for he has been preaching the pure Gospel, healing the sick, casting out demons, and bringing deliverance to the captives for many years. His book, *Finding God In Chaos*, is a reflection of his faith in which he tells readers that, even in the darkest hour...in the midst of chaos...they can find God, who can show them the way through their chaos.

Sometimes troubles and hardships happen to us to exhort us to call upon the Holy One who has known us from the foundations of the earth and who desires good—not evil—for us. This book will help you to be victorious over your trials and develop a deep faith that God is close to every one of us!

– Bishop Andrii Tyshchenko, *Senior Bishop of New Generation churches in Ukraine and Russia*

Introduction

Too many times over the course of a person's life, chaos comes busting in, causing disorder, fear, and madness. Occasionally, it gives fair warning that it's on its way. Other times it comes like a smack in the face. Know this: Chaos is a tool Satan uses to instill fear in your life and weaken your faith. Perhaps two of our worst fears are that things will get out of control and that God will abandon us.

Abandonment by God is the worst emotion any human could ever experience. It was the greatest of Jesus's agonies on the Cross. Matthew captures the moment: "And Jesus cried out with a loud voice, saying...My God, My God, why have You forsaken Me?" (Matthew 27:46, NKJV).

It's impossible for us to avoid chaos. But as a child of God, we do have a way of dealing with it. We simply transition our *fear* into *faith*.

Chaos Provides Us The Opportunity To See The Mighty Hand Of God Moving In Our Lives

The reality of your life as a Christian is that God is always with you. He promised to never leave you nor forsake you. God is right there in the middle of your chaos. He knows *everything* you are facing. He is only waiting for you to step out of the realm of the natural and into the realm of the Spirit, by exercising your faith. Nothing is impossible for God and He is always working out His plan for your life. He is forging an uncompromising spirit of faith that will propel you into your greatest calling. Through your tribulation, God is working in you a plan and purpose that is beyond your imagination. You must simply learn to *find* Him in the chaos and *trust* Him.

Great Things Are Birthed In Chaos
Destinies Are Forged In Chaos

Remember: "But without faith it is impossible to please Him, for he who comes to God must believe that He is, and that He is a rewarder of those who diligently seek Him" (Hebrews 11:6, NKJV). Our chaos provides us with the opportunity to see the mighty hand of God moving in our lives. With God, great things happen in chaos. Here is where He longs to show His greatness through you.

The following stories are about people confronting chaos. Read them thoughtfully. Reflect on each story, and gain a deep understanding of how God is always there in the midst of our chaos.

Whether it be a life and death situation, or just an annoying, stressful experience, our Heavenly Father cares for you and for every difficulty you face.

I pray these stories will inspire you to seek and discover God's presence when you find yourself in a tumultuous place. When you find yourself in chaos.

CHAPTER 1

———

Seek First

*"But seek first the kingdom of God
and His righteousness, and all these
things shall be added to you."*

MATHEW 6:33 NKJV

No Matter What, Seek First

The day my wife and I got married was the last time I saw Aaron alive. Aaron was my younger brother. The day, as you can imagine, was a time of great celebration for us, our families, and friends. It was a day of fun, joy, and a lot of laughter. A few days later, as my wife and I were returning home from our honeymoon, we were bumped up to first class. We were thrilled—a perfect ending to our perfect trip.

While sitting on the airplane, I began to reminisce about the last few days. Suddenly, I was overwhelmed by a wave of God's presence that was extremely powerful! Abruptly, the words of Matthew 6:33 came from deep within my heart: "But seek first the kingdom of God..." As I was caught up in this unique moment, the Lord began to impress on me the importance of seeking Him first, regardless of what the future might bring. I will always remember and treasure those words. I didn't know it, but at the time of my visitation, something was happening that would alter the rest of my life. It would become my worst day ever.

We finally arrived at our Northern Kentucky home in the Greater Cincinnati area. We'd been looking forward to being home again and to starting a new life together. Our first stop was at the home of my new in-laws. This was where all the gifts were from our wedding day. As we walked into the house, we looked around at all the gifts that had not been opened. Suddenly, the phone rang. It was my father. It was great to hear his voice and immediately I wanted to talk about our great trip. But he interrupted me.

"Mike, there has been an accident. Aaron was just killed." Upon hearing those words, I screamed out in denial, "No!"

God's Presence Can Always Be Found In Chaos

Aaron was killed in an automobile accident while traveling to my parents' new home in South Florida. Mom and Dad were driving down in a minivan. Aaron, along with my fourteen-year-old brother Isaac, was driving a small pickup truck. They had gotten as far as central Florida, when they found themselves engulfed in a sudden torrential downpour. Aaron was only seventeen and had not been driving long. He did not know how to handle a vehicle under those conditions. When he forcefully applied the brakes, it caused the small truck to hydroplane and Aaron lost control of the vehicle. As they slid alongside of my parents and sister, Aaron's truck began to flip. My parents witnessed him being thrown out of the driver side window. The pickup rolled over on him, and finally came to a stop, upside down.

Isaac quickly got out of the truck and raised his hands to heaven thanking God that he was okay, but he was unaware of what had happened to his brother. Aaron's body lay nearly lifeless in the pouring rain. When Isaac looked over and saw him, his praise to God turned into a surreal moment of fear and chaos. Mom quickly ran over to Aaron. She held him in her lap as the rain beat down on them, and she knew immediately that her son was not going to make it. Within minutes, she watched Aaron take his last breath.

Everything happened so quickly. Individuals from three cars who witnessed the accident pulled over and rushed to the scene. They came up to my mom as she held Aaron in her arms and asked what they could do to help. The only words she could say to them were, "Do you know Jesus? Do you know Jesus?" In the darkness of the moment, eternity was on my mom's mind. Her faith manifested. Yes, Aaron was gone, but Jesus was on the scene. So, she shared the Gospel with them.

In the weeks to come, my mom received three letters from some of the people who came to the scene to help. They wanted my mom to know that that day changed their lives. All three of them had come to know and accept Jesus because of the witness my mom shared. They saw a heart-torn mother embracing her dead son, yet her faith in Christ spoke to the eternal souls of those who had beheld the tragedy. In her grief, the words, "Do you know Jesus?" had pierced through the darkness and became words of hope, light, and life.

I had just gotten back from my honeymoon, so full of joy and excitement. Yet, in a moment's time, I began to experience one of the bleakest days of my life. Our wedding celebration was the last time I had seen Aaron alive. In the darkness of the moment I began to remember what had happened just two hours before. The words returned loud and strong. "No Matter What, Seek First!"

God knew. He had been waiting to speak to me at this particular moment, before I encountered my painful, life-altering experience. He was letting me know that He was aware of events about to happen, and no matter what, I should remember to "Seek Him and His kingdom first."

This experience was a shocking way to start a marriage, yet this was our reality. I found out later that the moment my brother had his accident was the same moment God visited me on the plane. I had no way of knowing that God was speaking to me in a moment of great chaos that I was nowhere near. What He shared with me that day would not only help get me through a very difficult time, but to this day, whenever I am faced with adversity, I am reminded of Matthew 6:33, "Seek First! No Matter What, Seek First!"

Seek First The Kingdom Of God

Life is full of ups and downs. My wife and I know firsthand the heartbreaking anguish that can arrive at a moment's notice and turn great joy into despair. So, it is imperative that we find God in our chaos because He is there. It is when we find Him that He can and will guide us out of the darkness and confusion. He will see us through the difficult hour of fear and chaos.

We all know that we will never understand why some of the things that happen in our lives happen. We know that we might not ever get the answer we so desperately want to one of life's most dreaded questions: "Why?" But there is one thing I do know, one thing I have learned. Before, during, and after the chaos, God is there! He has proven it time and time again. Knowing this truth, I choose to "Seek first!"

CHAPTER 2

The Melody of the Holy Ghost

*"But those who wait on the Lord shall renew
their strength; they shall mount up with wings
like eagles, they shall run and not be weary,
they shall walk and not faint."*

ISAIAH 40:31 NKJV

True Faith Waits Before God

Just because a person has faith doesn't mean he or she can't
ask God the hard questions. Life is too tragic in too many ways
for us to not ask them. My parents' faith and trust in God did
not waiver in the aftermath of my brother's tragic accident.
However, the pain of their child's death took a toll on them
emotionally. It is in times of great trial that people most often
lose faith. Faith begins to fade when the pain becomes too
overwhelming. Darkness takes its place, making it difficult to
see God in all the confusion. It is hard to have faith to believe
when we feel let down, discouraged, and forsaken.

Over the years I have dealt with many brokenhearted people. I have spent countless hours ministering to them. Life's problems became too much. They could not see God through their distress. Instead of drawing nearer to their heavenly Father, they became paralyzed in their weakness. They became overcome with confusion. The desire for an abundant life drifted away, along with the deep joys they once experienced when everything was going well.

It's easy to love God and pursue Him when all is well. It's easy to talk boldly about spiritual matters to those who are suffering, when you're not. But when we hurt, it's a whole other story. The true man and woman of God are the ones who remain faithful in adversity and chaos. They won't let go of God, even when things don't make sense. They are patient and enduring, even as the clouds move in and darkness envelopes their circumstances. Emotionally bankrupt, they continue pursuing God. They keep on pursuing because they know they cannot make it another day without God's strength. True faith waits before God. It is revealed when it is needed most—in the chaos. Then God answers, and the believer soars again. The weariness lifts. They only needed to wait on God.

Despite the loss of their child, my parents never lost their faith. They were broken in spirit, yet they knew God had not forsaken them. They continued to rely on the Lord daily for His strength and power.

While We Are Waiting, God Is Moving

About six months after my brother's death, my mom was not doing well. Her faith remained strong, but emotionally she was grieving and depressed. Even so, she and Dad faithfully went to church and honored the Lord in their lives. During one church service the minister said something that did not mean much to them at the time. The declaration was that, in the coming week, the Lord was going to bring a person into someone's life for a brief moment. That encounter would impact their struggle in a positive way.

A couple of days later my dad was, as usual, eating his breakfast and reading his Bible on the back porch. His heart was still very heavy from the death of Aaron. Like many times before, he cried out, "Lord, where are you?" He had been asking the Lord this hard question for some time. He was looking for comfort in a place where none seemingly could be found. He was worried about my mom's health. He also was wondering where Aaron was in eternity. My dad knew Aaron spent his teen years running from God. And while he was overjoyed that Aaron had turned to the Lord three months prior to his death, Dad wanted to know for sure. Did Aaron make it to heaven?

God Is Faithful To Those Who Wait On Him

To ease the turmoil raging inside his mind, my dad sought answers from God. Normally he would go in the house to pray, but that day he decided to stay outside. He cried out to God from the depths of his heart. He prayed in the Spirit and with his understanding. He paced back and forth, crying out loudly to God for the answer about his son. Dad never used Aaron's name while praying, but simply used the words "My son" in its place. "Lord, tell me about my son! Is he with You?"

21

Suddenly, while praying in the Spirit, he looked up and saw an African American man, a complete stranger. Dad took a second to gaze at this man standing, uninvited, in his back yard. He wondered, *What is this man doing?* My dad began to walk toward him. The stranger then announced loudly, "I was just passing by and I heard the melody of the Holy Ghost. I have come to tell you that Aaron went into the Holy of Holies. God is going to bless your children. He is going to bless your wife. He is going to bless your finances, thus saith the Lord."

Dad started to weep. He hugged the man and said, "My name is Mike." A reply came, "My name is John." Then Dad blessed him for his obedience in delivering this much-desired news.

In his chaos and pain, my dad sought God and found Him. God heard and answered his prayer. God did something supernatural to show not only my dad, but our entire family, that He is always close by. God is good! That day, God sent a man (or an angel?) to encourage my dad and reassure him that his son, Aaron, was in the presence of the Lord. On that day, joy began to fill our hearts. We knew God had not abandoned us. He showed us that Aaron was okay. God loved my dad enough to send a messenger into his back yard, and, as a result, my dad's heart and spirit once again began to soar like an eagle.

God is faithful when we cry out in our distress. He answers us when we call. Many people do not have the patience to wait for His answer. They can't find God in the chaos because they quit looking for Him. You must understand that God is in the chaos. Are you struggling with a challenging situation? Don't give up! Call upon the Lord in your time of need. Seek Him diligently. Be patient and wait on Him. God is not distant; He is very near. In His time, He will answer your prayers. Finding Him in the chaos can turn everything around in a moment. Then your strength will be renewed. You will mount up with wings like eagles. You will run and not be weary. You will walk and not faint.

CHAPTER 3

Heaven's Army

*"So He answered, 'Do not fear, for those who are
with us are more than those who are with them."*

2 KINGS 6:16 NKJV

Learn To Find God In Your Struggle

It is easy to have faith when everything is going well in
our lives, but what happens when the bottom drops out? What
happens when we are faced with uncertainty, and suddenly
our circumstances go from being filled with hope to complete
despair? What happens when we go from feeling like we're
in control to feeling confused and dismayed? Our response at
times like this exposes our faith—or lack of it. It is during the
most difficult times that the enemy of our faith will try to fill
our hearts and minds with doubt and unbelief. This is when he
uses fear as a weapon against the very essence of our faith. We
lose our ability to step out of the darkness by faith because we
allow our circumstances to become bigger than our faith.

At times like these we can be blinded to the revelation of truth, which is, God is still there! Where is there? In our chaos! He is waiting patiently for us to turn to Him, so He can guide us out of the darkness and confusion. True faith operates in the realm of the impossible. True faith is released when we have nothing to trust in but God. It begins when our strength ends, and His strength takes over.

In 2 Kings 6:8, the king of Syria made war against Israel. His plan was to set up military camps in strategic places to create havoc for Israel. With every move the Syrian king made, a recurring problem followed. Elisha, the Israeli prophet, heard from God about the Syrian king's war plans and would tell them to the king of Israel. Israel took the necessary measures to prevent being surprised and overtaken by the Syrians. This frustrated the king of Syria greatly, and he thought maybe one of his own soldiers was being disloyal and telling the king of Israel his plans. One of the Syrian king's servants spoke up and explained to him what was happening: "...Elisha, the prophet who is in Israel, tells the king of Israel the words that you speak in your bedroom" (2 Kings 6:12, NKJV).

Elisha's Faith Activated Heaven's Armies

God was using Elisha to help protect Israel. The Syrian king did not like this and sent a large army—including horses and chariots—to find and capture Elisha. The Syrian force discovered Elisha's location. Scripture says that they came at night and surrounded the city. In the morning, when Elisha's servant went outside and saw the great army that had surrounded the city, he immediately told Elisha what he saw.

Then the servant asked, "Oh no, my lord! What shall we do?" (2 Kings 6:15, NIV). Clearly, the servant saw an impossible situation. They were surrounded by the enemy and there was no way out. Yet in this dire situation Elisha speaks a word of faith. "Don't be afraid," the prophet answered. "Those who are with us are more than those who are with them" (2 Kings 6:16, NIV).

Imagine the servant's reaction to Elisha's words. "What, Elisha? Don't be afraid! We are surrounded by horses and chariots not to mention a great army! Elisha, there are only two of us and many of them. What are you talking about, 'don't be afraid?'" Knowing the servant could not see what he saw, Elisha prayed, "'Lord, I pray, open his eyes that he may see.' Then the Lord opened the eyes of the young man, and he saw. And behold, the mountain was full of horses and chariots of fire all around Elisha. So, when the Syrians came down to him, Elisha prayed to the Lord, and said, 'Strike this people, I pray, with blindness.' And He struck them with blindness according to the word of Elisha" (2 Kings 6:17-18 NKJV).

Not only did Elisha see into the supernatural, but God also allowed Elisha's servant to see, and then answered Elisha's prayer. The young man was able to witness the spiritual reality of the situation that God was with them ready to help. The servant saw that, although there was no way out of the situation in the natural, the spiritual reality was just the opposite. God was there in the chaos waiting to bring deliverance to His children.

Most of us are no different than Elisha's servant. Up to this point, I'm sure he had seen many demonstrations of the Lord working through Elisha. And, surely, the servant had heard about the wondrous works of God performed by Elisha's mentor, Elijah. While this young man's faith undoubtedly was developing and growing, his faith had been exposed by this situation. His response to his circumstance had been one of fear.

Throughout our lives, most of us find ourselves in similar situations—surrounded by a form of opposition that we can't seem to overcome. The good news is that this young man got to see the miraculous in his situation. The Lord used Elisha to encourage him when he was too weak to find the strength to call out to God on his own. Elisha, on the other hand, was a seasoned man of faith that was accustomed to seeing God's supernatural power. He grew to trust in the power of God regardless of the magnitude of opposition. He had a revelation that the physical, natural reality that we can see is not always the spiritual reality that exists in heaven's realm. Elisha's life had prepared him for this moment. He was able to see beyond the crisis. He was able to see the answer even before he called out in faith. And by his speaking out, Elisha's faith activated heaven's armies, and they immediately came to his and his servant's aid.

Faith Turns Chaos Into Opportunities

There will be times in our lives that our faith will be challenged greatly. Sometimes, like the young man, we might be weak in our moment of trial. At such times, God wants to teach us to reach out to Him regardless of our miserable condition. He wants to teach us to turn our fear into faith. He wants us to be more like Elisha, who was able to trust Him in

28

the difficult hour. Elisha had the revelation that, indeed, God was there the whole time of this confrontation. He could see what others could not.

God was there when the Syrian army, with horses and chariots, surrounded Elisha. God was there waiting to rescue His servants from the hands of the enemy. He was there in the chaos longing to demonstrate His greatness over the powers of darkness. God wants us to know that He is there with us in our difficult hour when the future seems uncertain. He is there ready to bring His deliverance to us in our time of need.

Let us learn to be more like Elisha and see beyond our circumstances. Let us, by faith, learn to find God in our struggle, for He is there in our chaos.

CHAPTER 4

Jesus! Help Me!

"Because he loves me," says the Lord,
"I will rescue him; I will protect him,
for he acknowledges my name.
He will call on me, and I will answer him;
I will be with him in trouble,
I will deliver him and honor him."

PSALM 91:14-15 NIV

Christ In Us Is The Victory

When I was a young pastor, the Lord had already placed a burden on my heart for the nations. I had been at my new church for only a few months when people began to have supernatural experiences like healings and deliverances. Even so, I strongly desired to learn more about God's plans for me. One day, my phone rang. It was another pastor. He called me to ask if I would be willing to help lead a team of college students to India. The mission was to help establish a new church in the city of Mumbai. I knew the request was of the Lord because two years earlier I started to have a strong desire to minister in India. I agreed to go and started looking forward to the mission trip. Up to this point, I had been on other mission outings, but never to India. Though I didn't know it at the time, God was going to use this trip to humble me and teach me some valuable lessons.

Many people get excited when God chooses to use them for His purpose and I was no different. But in our immaturity and lack of true experiences, we can become arrogant. Americans, especially on their first international mission trip, can be very prideful in their thinking. "I'll go to these countries and teach them a thing or two about the powers of darkness and the supernatural power of God," they tell themselves.

I view this attitude as arrogant American faith. Thank God, even in our stupidity, He shows us grace. Fortunately, very soon, I would begin to see the world differently. My American faith would be challenged, and I would find myself facing a reality to which I was not accustomed.

We Must Walk Humbly Trusting In The Power Of Christ

India was extremely different from any place I had ever been. Let me explain. The United States has a history of being a Christian nation. Because of its Christ-centered heritage of faith and prayer, America has experienced some protection from the onslaught of evil, demonic forces. It is almost as if a spiritual shield has covered our nation. India has had no such shield. A very small percentage of its population is Christian. The overwhelming majority of its people practice Hinduism. This leaves India (and other non-Christian nations) wide open to spiritual attack and influence by demonic principalities and the powers of darkness.

Most people, including those who consider themselves of the Christian faith, don't realize there is a very real devil who wants to devour us. Every one of us has a bullseye on our forehead, and Satan's aim is to bring chaos not only into the world but also into our lives. Satan uses every weakness we have as humans and as individuals to devise personal attacks and temptations against us. Chaos and fear are two of his favorite battle weapons. Pastors, missionaries, evangelists, and others who actively work to spread the gospel are not immune. Jesus told Peter in Luke 22:31, "Simon, Simon, behold, Satan hath desired to have you, that he may sift you as wheat" (KJV). When hell shows up to challenge our faith, we must learn to call on God quickly lest a paralyzing fear overcomes our faith.

We finally arrived in Mumbai, India. There were about twenty people in our team. When we reached our sleeping quarters, we were two rooms short. I was asked to take two of the young men with me and go to another place for the duration of the trip. We quickly walked the half mile to our new accommodations. My room was directly above the students' room. On the second night, I was fast asleep. Around 3:00 a.m., I woke up, unable to breathe. It was as if I was being choked by something. The door to my room was shaking and yet there was no one at the door. I finally realized a demonic spirit was attacking me. Immediately, a fear like I've never felt before gripped me. I was surrounded by a dark, frightening presence and I was gasping for breath.

My body...my mind...went from peaceful slumber to terrifying chaos in a moment. I wish I could say I just stood up and began to command that thing—that spirit—to stop and get out in the name of Jesus! That's what I'd always thought I would do. But it's also easy to think that when you're not being attacked. It's easy to say when you live in a bubble. Honestly, at that instant, my arrogant American faith could not kick in. I was too weak, too scared, and too overpowered by fear to say anything. In my weakness...in the darkness...in my chaos...the only words I could manage to mutter were, "Jesus, help me!" As soon as I spoke those words, my breathing returned to normal and the fear quickly faded from the room.

Within a minute, all the fear, darkness, and chaos were gone, and a complete peace now filled the room. The peace was so soothing that I quickly fell asleep again. But it was only a matter of minutes before my phone rang. It was one of the college students in the room below me. He was panicking and shouting, "Pastor Mike, get down here right away. We are under attack! Please HELP!"

Christ In Us Gives Us The Victory

Hearing those words and his tone, I knew exactly what was happening. That same demon of fear had just passed through my room. I got to their room as quickly as I could. When I walked into the room, one of the students, sitting on his bed with his hands over his ears convulsing, rocked back and forth screaming, "I'm being attacked, help me!" We began calling on the name of Jesus. A few minutes later, the young man stopped his convulsing and began to weep. "It's gone," he said. "It's gone." That morning, we experienced a very real attack from a very real demonic spirit. It did not care that we were saved by

34

the blood of Jesus Christ. It wanted to saddle us with a spirit of fear to hinder the advancement of the gospel.

I learned a valuable lesson about myself that day. My Americanized faith was not as strong as I'd thought. I'd been too weak to fight through the chaos on my own. I'd been briefly overpowered by a force greater than myself. But in the chaos of that early morning, I learned something I'll never forget: We must walk humbly trusting in the power of Christ.

CHAPTER 5

The Miracle Patient

"In the day of my trouble
I will call upon You,
For You will answer me."

PSALM 86:7 NKJV

God Cares Enough To Answer Our Prayers

One Sunday morning a married couple walked into our church. Up to this point, they had not attended church services anywhere. Lee, a friend of mine from the church, had invited them. He knew they were going through an extremely difficult time and needed a miracle. A few minutes before the service started, I was introduced to Pam and Rick.

Pam's face showed of desperation. Rick was sitting in a chair, a cold look of despair and pain engulfing him. Pam wasted no time in sharing their need—Rick was dying, with only a few weeks to live. He needed a liver transplant right away. She said the doctors would not put him on the transplant list because he also had cancer. For Rick to be put on the transplant list, he had to be cancer free. Any kind of treatment such as chemotherapy had been ruled out; his liver's critical condition made his body too weak. Simply stated, he was a dead man walking.

With this brief introduction to Rick's health issues, Pam asked if we would pray for the cancer to be healed so Rick could be placed on the transplant list. That is what she asked for, and that is what we did. We prayed a simple, but direct, prayer of faith that the cancer would be supernaturally healed.

A week later, Pam and Rick were at the church. She held a big envelope and came over to me with a grin on her face. Pam told me Rick's cancer was gone. She opened the big envelope in front of me and pulled out an MRI picture to show me the evidence. The doctors could not believe what they saw, she said. The cancer, in a matter of a few days, had disappeared. The doctors asked Pam and Rick what happened. Pam told me she looked at them and said, "Jesus healed the cancer." This, indeed, was a miracle. God answered our simple prayer of faith. This miracle opened the door for Rick to be added to the transplant list.

A couple of weeks after that, Pam and Rick showed up at church. Rick was looking even worse and obviously losing weight. Pam came up to me and asked me to pray again. The need was literally life and death. Rick needed a new liver now!

The Lord Responds To The Cries Of His Children

Again, we prayed for God to intervene in Rick's dire situation. Again, the Lord heard our humble prayer. Minutes later during the morning service, Pam received word that a liver had been found for Rick. Rick was scheduled for surgery immediately. The surgery appeared to go exactly as planned. Pam was thankful that things were working out so well for her husband. Only a few weeks earlier, Pam and Rick had had no hope. Now, Pam was gleaming as her husband came out of surgery. The doctor told Pam it was a miracle Rick had not died months ago because, when they removed the old liver, it fell apart like jelly. Pam was thankful for her new-found faith in Christ and how He cared enough to answer our prayers.

Unfortunately, her joy did not last long. Two days after his surgery, Rick's vital signs changed drastically for the worse. The doctors examined Rick, hoping to discover what was going on. A short time later, they discovered Rick was bleeding internally. The doctors forewarned Pam that the surgery might be lengthy because they were not sure where Rick was bleeding and had no idea how bad it would be. Pam feared for her husband's life. Once again, she reached out for prayer. I was out of town when my phone rang. When I answered, Pam was frantically shouting that her husband was in trouble again. The doctors had told her they needed to find the bleeding fast because the longer Rick laid on the table, the more dangerous things became. She asked me to pray the doctors would identify the bleeding quickly. Once more, I said a modest prayer, asking only what Pam requested.

The doctors and the nurses preparing Rick for anesthesia. Pam, at this point, was a wreck after all she had endured the past few weeks. She wanted another prayer—and now—before she would let them operate on her husband. She knew God had come through each time before and she needed him to come through this time as well. Knowing that I was out of town, Pam called my friend, Lee. Lee was aware of Rick's situation. He was sitting in the parking lot of a home builder store when his phone rang. He answered, and Pam frantically told him of the grim situation. Lee didn't know it at the time, but she had activated the speaker phone for all to hear.

Lee began to pray that the Lord would not only be with Rick, but he began to intercede for the doctors and nurses as well. He prayed that the doctors would supernaturally find the problem and soon. Knowing that Rick could die on the operating table, the doctors and nurses bowed their heads when they heard Lee praying. Suddenly, the glory of the Lord filled the room. The surgical team began to cry as they sensed the Lord's presence. A sudden peace came over Pam and the doctors and nurses momentarily wondered what had just happened.

The surgical team began its work. Once more, the Lord answered a simple prayer. The doctors found the location of the internal bleeding immediately and repaired it. They were astonished at how readily they found the bleeding. They knew what they'd experienced was not normal and remembered Lee's prayer. Rick's doctor, who had been seeing him from the start, was amazed. He'd seen Rick go through some major hurdles in the space of a few weeks, and he was still alive. He began to call Rick his "miracle patient."

God Is In The Chaos Working Out His Will

Pam thanked God for answered prayers. She called me and shared how God worked through the surgical team. She told me how God came in the room when Lee prayed and how the team began to cry. She was happy and filled with joy. It was as if peace finally had come.

The doctors were pleased with the transplant and relieved the bleeding had stopped. Rick's body had been through a lot, but now they believed everything looked good. He rested as his body slowly recovered from the trauma. At this point, Rick had had three miracles take place as God answered prayer requests in life-threatening, chaotic moments. About 48 hours later my phone rang. It was Pam.

CHAPTER 6

Keep Praying

"But certainly, God has heard me;
He has attended to the voice of my prayer."

PSALM 66:19 NKJV

God Is In The Midst Of Chaos

I was back in town when Pam called this time. Rick's body was shutting down, and his vital signs were at dangerous levels. It had nothing to do with the previous surgeries. As far as the doctors could tell, all those obstacles had been resolved. They had no clue as to what was happening. The doctors ordered an MRI that showed exactly what was wrong. The new liver had somehow twisted in a 90-degree angle causing it not to work properly. The hospital consulted five of the best doctors in the country searching for answers. After evaluating the situation, the doctors determined that nothing else could be done.

The possibility of another surgery was not even an option. They were certain that Rick would die on the operating table after having had two major surgeries back to back. They noted that nobody had ever survived this type of complication. Rick was in a no-win situation. Rick was going to die and there was nothing else anybody could do to help him. This news was devastating, especially knowing that it came from some of the best medical minds in the United States.

At this news, Pam's mind snapped. Enough was enough. She looked at her husband's body, knowing this time it truly was over. Despite the miracles she had witnessed the last couple of weeks, her newfound faith weakened. Dark thoughts took over her mind. All the turmoil of this entire ordeal had reached its limit. Chaos had won. In this dark moment, Pam made a rash decision. It was as if something evil had overtaken her. Pam walked over to Rick's bedside to say goodbye. Then, abruptly, she left the room. Like a zombie, she walked through the hallways of the hospital. She made her way outside. She had decided to step out in front of a city bus. She was determined to end her life.

God's Intervening Hand

She moved to the edge of the sidewalk as a bus approached. As the bus was about to reach her, her leg moved forward to take her final step in this world. Suddenly, she felt a hand pull her back from the bus. As soon as that happened, she snapped back to her right mind. Pam looked around to see who saved her. There wasn't a single person near her. The supernatural hand of the Lord had stopped her.

Quickly, Pam went back to her husband's room. When she arrived, there was a nurse in the room. The nurse looked different. This nurse wasn't wearing scrubs. She wore a traditional nurse's uniform and cap—the kind they wore years ago. Pam was perplexed at this woman's presence and wondered why she was there. The peculiar nurse began to speak of how Rick was not going to die, but live. Then the nurse disappeared. Pam was now even more perplexed and wondered if she had encountered an angel?

Pam called me. She told me there was a complication, and the doctors said Rick was going to die. When I heard this, I headed straight to the hospital. While I was driving, I pondered this bizarre and unusual chain of events. I considered how God had performed three miracles when we prayed. He healed Rick's cancer, so he could be put on the transplant list and provided a liver literally within minutes after we prayed for one. Then, Rick's doctors had a supernatural encounter with God's presence and they were able to quickly identify the location of Rick's internal bleeding. Three miracles and yet his death was now imminent? That didn't sit well with me. I began to pray and as I prayed I thought how God would not have done all this just to let Rick die. I could not accept that.

I arrived at the hospital and went to Rick's room. Pam looked dazed and very confused. She said the doctors had just left. They told her she needed to let Rick go. He had no chance of pulling through this. He was dying. Suddenly, boldness came over me and I looked at Pam, and I said, "Let's pray." I walked over to Rick's bedside and looked at his seemingly lifeless body. I grabbed his cold hand as he laid there unresponsive. I began to pray, but this time my prayer was different. I prayed not only for his healing but also for his deliverance.

The Holy Spirit had opened my eyes to this whole situation. This ordeal was connected to a demonic spirit of death. This spirit kept trying to kill Rick, but each time we prayed the spirit's power was broken. I started by taking authority over the spirit of death in Rick's life and commanded it to release him in Jesus's name. I began to pray life back into Rick's body. It was not a long prayer, but it was very direct.

After the prayer, I did not linger in the room. I simply encouraged Pam and walked out. Within two hours, Pam called me. Her voice was full of joy and excitement. "Pastor Mike, right after you left the room, life began to come back to Rick's body," she said. "His vital signs started climbing."

"The people at the hospital are trying to figure out what happened," she continued. "A doctor just came in, and he does not understand what's going on. They are all bewildered knowing that Rick should be a dead man. They are ordering more tests to find out what happened, but I know Jesus has healed him!"

The doctors ordered another MRI. To their amazement, they learned that not only was the liver in perfect position, but the picture also revealed something that looked like a hand holding the liver.

God Saves, Heals, And Delivers

The doctors were amazed once more by their patient's medical journey. Pam's faith came back in full. News of this miracle spread around the hospital quickly. Nurses and doctors from other departments wanted to stop by and meet the miracle patient. Whenever they came in, Pam was quick to tell them that Jesus healed him.

Rick's recovery from this point was unusually quick. He went home within a few days. Rick not only survived his chaotic ordeal, but he was the first person in medical history to survive this type of medical condition. It was so miraculous that the lead doctor, one of the very best in the world, asked permission to document and publicize Rick's story in a medical journal. This doctor continues to use Rick's story as an example of medical mysteries and miracles. The doctor still calls Rick his miracle patient.

Pam and Rick's story is a story of hope in chaos. Again and again, devastating setbacks and obstacles arose, yet God was there the entire time. He was there drawing them to Him in their time of great need. My friend, Lee, knew they needed God's help. When he invited them to church, he opened a door for them to reach out to God. The moment they accepted the invitation was the moment they began to seek God and cast their cares upon Him. It was in that moment they began to discover God in the midst of their chaos.

If Pam and Rick had never come to church that day, Rick would have died. As they reached out to God in their chaos, they found Him. He was there. And they learned He is the God that saves, heals, and delivers.

CHAPTER 7

God's in the Crazy

*"Trust in the Lord with all your heart,
And lean not on your own understanding."*

PROVERBS 3:5 NKJV

Always Pursue The Heart Of God

I go and minister to the nations today because God, in the past, brought the nations to me. Out of the relationships I developed with people of other cultures, God opened the door for me to minister in other nations. While I was still serving as a pastor, several of the people attending my church were of different nationalities. God was moving with signs and wonders in our church, and many people experienced healing and deliverance. Because of what the Lord was doing in their lives, many of these foreigners would invite others from the same background to the church.

Over time, I felt a strong urge to minister to the nations more frequently. Early on I was blessed to have some families from Trinidad. I told Jerry, my friend from Trinidad, that we needed to go to his homeland; all we needed was an open door. Several families from this Southern Caribbean island attended my church. I knew there was a great need for ministry in Trinidad. Despite these families and their connections back home, a door never opened for us to go there. Nonetheless, I continued to declare we needed God to open a door in Trinidad. We were patient, trusting in the Lord to make this trip happen in His good time. Then it happened. Jerry called me. He was ecstatic. "Pastor, you're not going to believe what happened!" he exclaimed. "We need to meet right away."

We got together, and he told me this incredible story. Around 11 p.m., his three-year-old grandson had been playing with his cell phone, pressing the numbers at random. A few minutes later Jerry's cell phone rang, and he answered it. The voice on the other end said, "Hello, you just called this number and I am calling you back."

"I'm sorry," Jerry explained, "My grandson was just playing with my phone and I guess he accidentally dialed your number."

"This is a private number," said the voice on the other line. "I see that you are calling me from the United Sates. I am a pastor in Trinidad." This got Jerry's attention fast!

"Really!" he said. "I'm a believer here in the States."

They talked for a while and Jerry told him how I had been trusting God to open a door for ministry in Trinidad. Both men were amazed by this incident of the accidental phone call. It was supernatural. Jerry suggested that Luke, the pastor from Trinidad, call me.

God Is In The Chaos Directing Our Paths

A few days later Luke did call me. We had a great conversation but did not make any plans at the time. We talked and discovered that our ministries had a lot in common. Sometime later we learned that when the phone rang that night, Pastor Luke and his wife were in bed. It only rang twice and by the time Luke got to his phone, the call had disconnected. His wife asked who it was. Luke said he didn't know, but noted it was a call from the United States. Luke headed back to bed, but his wife said, "You need to call that number back now!" Luke reluctantly called the number back and Jerry answered.

Several months later Pastor Luke came to the United States to minister at a church. He was so moved by the supernatural phone call he decided to fly to the Greater Cincinnati area just to meet Jerry and myself.

The pastor whose church Luke had visited said he thought Luke was crazy to visit people he had never met. After all, the only connection was a crazy, accidental phone call. But Pastor Luke felt prompted by the Holy Spirit to come and meet us after the night of the phone call. Jerry and I had no part in setting up the meeting.

God Can Be Found In The Crazy

When Pastor Luke arrived, Jerry met him at the airport. We all enjoyed a wonderful lunch together. There wasn't any agenda other than to connect and hear what the Lord was doing in our lives, our churches, and our communities. Immediately, we sensed the Lord was in our presence. As we shared our hearts with one another, it was obvious the Lord had a bigger plan in mind. By the end of our lunch, Pastor Luke invited us to minister at his church in Trinidad. Three months later, we arrived in Trinidad. We had some powerful services in numerous churches. God displayed His awesome power and many people experienced healing and deliverance. All of this came about because of a three-year-old child's accidental phone call and it continues to amaze me. If God wants to do something in our lives, He will make it happen.

He is the one that is truly in control regardless of any and all obstacles. We simply need to yield to His purpose. If He is able to open doors to the nations supernaturally, surely He can do the same in your everyday situations.

Because of Pastor Luke's faithfulness to follow God's leading and our visit to Trinidad, God made available to me other nations and divine relationships that continue to bear fruit today. God wanted me not only to go to Trinidad, but also many other nations. Who could have guessed that one divine phone call would result in so much international ministry? It seems crazy.

Sometimes that is where we'll find God—in the crazy. He has a plan; we just need to continue to pursue His heart. As we pursue Him, He always finds a way to make something awesome out of crazy.

CHAPTER 8

The Kneeling Jihadist

"He performs wonders that cannot be fathomed,
miracles that cannot be counted."

JOB 5:9 NKJV

God's People Are Everywhere

As I have traveled around the world I've had the privilege of meeting great men and women of God. These people have incredible stories of God's miraculous wonders. They are people who will never be of international renown, yet they are known in heaven. I've had the pleasure of knowing Muslims who have come to Christ because Jesus showed up in a vision. I've met believers who have been beaten and tortured for their faith. I've been with people who have had relatives imprisoned for years and still will not renounce Christ. It is very humbling and stirring to hear how these amazing people responded in the chaos—surrounded by darkness and the possibility of paying the ultimate price—their lives.

Another story I would like to share is about my friend from India, who I met on one of my trips. Prior to accepting Christ as his savior, Ramesh was a very successful business man. In fact, he had become a millionaire. He took a job in a Muslim country and great things were happening for him. Then it happened. Ramesh had an encounter with Jesus that changed his life. Immediately, he was on fire for the things of God. He longed to see others come to the saving knowledge of Jesus, just as he had. However, he was living in a Muslim nation where it was illegal to talk about Jesus.

Shortly after coming to Christ, Ramesh started losing all his money. Yet it did not deter him or his newfound faith in Christ. He discovered that Jesus was more important than the riches of this world. The hardships Ramesh faced only drew him closer to Jesus. He longed to give his life to making Jesus known wherever the Lord led him. It was not long before his zeal landed him in a difficult situation. He was led by the Lord to share his faith with a man who happened to be a devout Muslim. This man contacted the police and Ramesh was quickly arrested. He was incarcerated with dangerous criminals who were accused of major crimes.

Not long after Ramesh was put in prison, he saw a young man weeping because he was in great pain. Feeling compassion, Ramesh asked the guards if they could get the man some medical attention. When no one would help, Ramesh approached him and recognized his ailment. He had a thyroid condition and his throat was extremely swollen.

God Is In The Chaos Performing His Will

It was then the Holy Spirit told Ramesh to lay hands on this prisoner's throat and plead the blood of Jesus Christ over him. Ramesh asked the young man for his permission to pray for his healing. The man quickly agreed, thankful that someone was willing to do something. Ramesh stretched forth his hand to the young man's throat and prayed. The power of God manifested in him, and he fell to the ground unconscious. Several prisoners and guards watched as all of this took place. The guards thought Ramesh tried to strangle the man and quickly rushed in to see what Ramesh had done.

By the time the guards made it over to the man, he started to get up. He stood to his feet and professed he was healed. He noticed all the pain and swelling was gone. The Lord supernaturally healed him in front of all the guards and inmates. Ramesh and the young man gave thanks to the Lord Jesus Christ. No one who saw what took place could believe what had just happened. Only a few minutes ago this man had been in extreme pain. Indeed, it was a miracle.

When We Are Weak God Shows Himself Strong

This frustrated the guards and the police officers who were present. They were all devout Muslims and despised Christianity. Because of Ramesh's obedience to pray for this sick young man, many prisoners were converting to Christianity and accepting Jesus Christ as Lord and Savior. The prison administration decided it had to punish Ramesh for converting all these Muslims to Jesus. The guards came in and removed him from all the other prisoners and placed him in an isolated cell, so he could not cause any more disturbances. Ramesh's new cell had one other inmate—a devout Muslim. After a couple of hours of silence, the two started making small talk, which, ultimately, turned into a debate about Christianity and Islam. The Muslim emphatically defended Islam while Ramesh defended his faith, striving to prove that Jesus Christ alone is the way, truth, and life. This spirited debate lasted three days. After three days, the young man whom Jesus healed was released. He requested to visit Ramesh for a few minutes. The guards brought Ramesh to him for a brief goodbye.

In those few moments, the young man expressed his thanks to Ramesh. He was very grateful for what Ramesh had done. Then, just before he left, he said something that terrified Ramesh, concerning his cell mate. When Ramesh was taken back to his cell, his countenance was different. Ramesh would not talk to or even look at his cell mate. It was obvious to the Muslim man that Ramesh was very troubled. The man asked Ramesh what was wrong. Ramesh ignored him. The man insisted that Ramesh answer him. In a voice quivering with fear, Ramesh reluctantly asked, "Are you a Jihadi terrorist who killed one hundred people?" Proudly, the man responded, "No, one hundred and sixty people!" When Ramesh heard this, he was petrified. He had just spent the last three days trying to convince a radical jihadist that his religion is not the right way to heaven and that Jesus Christ is the only true Lord and Savior. Now he was concerned for his safety within his own prison cell.

Ramesh's previous boldness disintegrated. His boldness for the Lord—the very reason he was in this situation—turned into confusion and despair. His humanity exposed, he now cowered in the corner hoping to survive. In this dark place, Ramesh did his best to pull himself together. In silence, he cried out to the Lord for strength. Suddenly, the Holy Spirit came upon Ramesh. His eyes closed and he felt the overwhelming presence of God. The Holy Spirit began to speak through Ramesh in a language he did not know. It was so powerful that he could not stop praying. He could not even open his eyes.

Ramesh's prayer did not last long. When he opened his eyes, he was astonished at what he saw. Kneeling before him was the Muslim jihadist, tears streaming down his face. The man then asked Ramesh, "How did you know everything I have ever done in this life? And how can you speak Pashto?" (Pashto was his native language in Afghanistan.) Ramesh looked directly at him and responded, "It was not me, but the Lord Jesus Christ who spoke to you through the power of the Holy Spirit."

God Performs Wonders That Cannot Be Fathomed

At this, the jihadist repented of all his sins and gave his life to Jesus Christ. The Holy Spirit told Ramesh to tell him that he would be extradited to a country where he would receive his punishment for his crimes. The Muslim-turned-Christian was thankful to the Lord Jesus Christ for saving him. It was the first time in his life he had experienced true peace. He could now move forward, even knowing he faced the possibility of execution. He now had the confidence that his sins were forgiven and was convinced that Jesus Christ was Lord of all.

The next day, the guards came to take the man away. As he was leaving, he looked at Ramesh and said, "Brother, we will meet again in the presence of the Lord." Ramesh prayed with him one last time, and then he was carted off. Shortly thereafter, by the grace of God, Ramesh was released. He was deported and forbidden to ever enter the country again. Ramesh currently lives in a safe place doing his best to advance the gospel of Jesus Christ.

This story is filled with the handprint of Jesus. Because God so loved Ramesh and the Muslims in that prison, He allowed chaos to fall upon Ramesh. In that chaos, God sent a light into the darkness. In a prison, a young man was supernaturally healed resulting in many Muslims accepting Christ. In addition, a murdering jihadist came to accept that same saving faith prior to his potential execution. God is in the chaos performing His will, not wanting any to perish but wanting all men to repent, believe, and be saved.

CHAPTER 9

Going to the Other Side

That day when evening came,
he said to his disciples,
"Let us go over to the other side."

MARK 4:35 NIV

In Our Troubles, God's Will Shall Prevail

I received an invitation to minister in a Middle Eastern Muslim nation where they practice sharia law. This opportunity came about because of Ramesh. On one of my previous trips, Ramesh was moved by what he had witnessed in the services. He wanted me to go to this country—the one where he had been imprisoned—to minister. He told me that a ministry like mine was greatly needed in that part of the world. He knew of a ministry there, made the connection with the church, and the details were worked out.

Knowing where I was headed, I learned what I should and shouldn't do on matters such as immigration upon arrival and the everyday customs of the people. I couldn't afford to make a mistake that might get me arrested or offend the entire population. Prior to my leaving, a friend connected me with an acquaintance of hers who worked at the airport where I'd be landing. I was grateful for this because I was already a bit nervous. This was my first trip to this region, and it didn't help that I was by myself. Nevertheless, I had learned to just keep moving forward by faith and trust in God's protection.

When the plane landed, and the doors opened, I heard my name over the aircraft's loud speakers. I was directed to meet this person upon exiting the plane. He was a manager at one of the airlines in that city. He also is a Christian, and he wanted to help me through customs and do his best to protect me until I found the pastor hosting me. While all the passengers followed the signs to customs, he led me in a different direction. We skipped around the lines to a place where VIPs entered the country, and border agents didn't ask any questions. For me, this was wonderful as I would not have to give an account of myself or my reason for being there. I made it through customs and, eventually, found the pastor and those with him. They took me to the hotel and gave me a rundown of the agenda for the week ahead.

The pastor I met was not native to the nation where we both were now. He had come to this country nine years earlier to start a church. Since he had arrived, he was never allowed to go back home—not even to visit his family. He was stuck there. But while he was stuck there, God's favor rested upon him. He started a powerful ministry and impacted many lives with the Gospel of Jesus Christ in a place where you dare not talk about Jesus outside the walls of your property.

Faith Embraces The Will Of God

Our first service was wonderful. The Lord moved in a mighty way and lives were greatly touched. When our service ended, we reminded the people that the next service would be in a few days. We talked about what we believed the Lord wanted to do in the next meeting, and the people received it with great anticipation.

On Sunday night, some of the key leaders of the church gathered in an apartment for their weekly meeting. Since I was there, the pastor asked me to teach on kingdom principles. Afterward, we prayed for the individuals who were present. Then the Lord's presence entered the room like a fire. The Lord gave me a prophetic word for the pastor. God was going to change the focus of his ministry. The pastor would minister to thousands of people, and God would confirm His word with signs and wonders.

The next day I noticed the pastor seemed a little distant and very worried. I knew something was going wrong, but I was not sure what it was. I did not ask him because I did not know the man that well. I figured if he wanted me to know something, he would tell me. Two days later, one of the church leaders called me and said that something had happened to his pastor. He said he would meet me at the hotel in a couple of hours to discuss the situation. I had no idea what had happened.

God Sees Beyond The Chaos

I waited patiently until the pastor's right-hand man arrived. We sat down and then he told me the pastor had been arrested and was in jail. One of the Muslim leaders had turned him in, knowing he was a Christian. The next day we did not hear anything new concerning the pastor. At this point, all the church could do was hope and pray for his speedy release. Everyone continued to trust God in this situation. All I could think about was his wife and children. How does anyone handle something like this? What about the congregation? How do they cope with such uncertainty? I had heard of things like this happening in Muslim countries, but this time I was a part of the story.

In a few hours, I would be called upon to preach to a church filled with believers who were heartbroken about the plight of their pastor. What could I say to these people? This whole situation was unnerving. Here I was, the guest minister of a Christian church in a Muslim country, the church's pastor was in jail, and the congregation was alarmed for his and their safety! These were dark and chaotic circumstances.

In such a time as this, you need to turn your attention to the Lord. You must pursue Him for His supernatural peace. You must search for Him in the chaos. I thought about that evening in my hotel room when I prophesied over the pastor. As I considered this, I remembered what the Lord had said to him. I also thought about how nervous and distant he had acted the following day. It was as if he knew something was getting ready to happen but had no clue as to what. It seemed he knew trouble was forthcoming, and the outcome was uncertain.

As I considered everything that had taken place the past few days, the Lord guided my thoughts to a certain passage of scripture, and I could not get it out of my head. I knew it was of God and that I had to share His word with the church that evening. The scripture was from Mark 4:35-41, NIV:

> That day when evening came, he said to his disciples, "Let us go over to the other side." Leaving the crowd behind, they took him along, just as he was, in the boat. There were also other boats with him. A furious squall came up, and the waves broke over the boat, so that it was nearly swamped. Jesus was in the stern, sleeping on a cushion. The disciples woke him and said to him, "Teacher, don't you care if we drown?"
>
> He got up, rebuked the wind and said to the waves, "Quiet! Be still!" Then the wind died down and it was completely calm. He said to his disciples, "Why are you so afraid? Do you still have no faith?" They were terrified and asked each other, "Who is this? Even the wind and the waves obey him!"

Have you ever been in a situation or trial and felt as if God wasn't hearing your prayers or, worse, that He just didn't care? It is in such difficult times as these that many people lose faith. They have great difficulty trusting God during the storms of life and the chaos brought by them.

In this gospel story, the disciples were very afraid, even though Jesus was in the boat with them. But in their fear... in the chaos...they still called upon Jesus to help them in their time of trouble. It was as if Jesus was waiting on them to call before He responded and brought them peace. They found God in the chaos that night.

After Jesus rebuked the wind and the waves, He asked the disciples a pointed question: "Why are you so afraid? Do you still have no faith?" Jesus was trying to get them to understand that He had already spoken faith into their hearts before they got in the boat when He said, "Let us go over to the other side." The disciples learned a valuable lesson that day. We are to live by faith. Jesus expected that of them—and us. Even so, when our faith doesn't measure up to the storms and chaos of life, then we can call upon the name of Jesus and know He is right there with us.

At last, the time for the church service came around. Many of the people were extremely sad and apprehensive because of the grave situation. But it didn't take long for God's presence to come in and shift the entire meeting. When it was time for me to preach, boldness rose up in me. I began to explain how God was getting ready to do something great with their pastor's life. Jesus already had spoken faith into his dire situation before the arrest. Jesus had already told him that he was going to the other side. That night, God moved with great power. Everyone knew that He was with them and in control of their pastor's circumstances. The Lord confirmed His word with multiple signs and wonders. The church leaders who were present said they had never had such a service as this one. They had never before witnessed the things they saw that night.

God's Will Is Revealed Through Chaos

The hand of God was something to behold that night. He encouraged an entire church as well as the pastor's wife and children. So, what was the outcome for the pastor? A few days later, he was forced to leave the country without his wife and children. After nine long years of being unable to leave the country on his own accord, the pastor found God in the chaos. Men deported him, but God promoted him.

The pastor was sent to India, his homeland. He had not seen his family in nine years and had missed his father's funeral years earlier. But now, by the mighty hand and grace of God, he was supernaturally reunited with his mother and siblings. Upon his arrival home, many church leaders in India reached out to him. He immediately began to preach to the masses. In the first couple of months, the pastor held over fifty meetings and the scheduling did not stop. Through his ministry, multiple thousands have been saved, healed, and delivered.

The leaders from the pastor's former church started to shoulder their share of the ministry along with the pastor's wife. The church continued to flourish despite the whole ordeal. But now, looking back, everyone knows that God was in the chaos working out His perfect will.

Even though a giant ministry was birthed out of this pastor's trial, it still was not easy for him as the ordeal continued; the pastor was still separated from his wife and children for a time. His family was, however, eventually reunited with him in India.

Sometimes Jesus allows things to happen that are way outside of our comfort zone. And yet, it is the only way for His will to come to pass. It is in these challenging times that our faith is tested. When we are going through the storms and chaos of life, we don't have to live in fear or doubt because we know Jesus is with us and is taking us to the other side.

CHAPTER 10

As Petty as an Airline Seat

"For I know the plans I have for you,"
declares the Lord,
"plans to prosper you and not to harm you,
plans to give you hope and a future."
JEREMIAH 29:11 NIV

We Move Forward By Faith

I received an invitation to minister in Ghana, Africa, and gladly accepted it. Prior to my arrival, I was told the meetings would be advertised all over the city. They sent me a copy of the ad and upon looking at it, I laughed. It read, "Seven Day Encounter from Demonic Curses, Evil Covenants, Yokes of Bondage, and Powers of Witchcraft." While preparing for my trip, I learned that the witches in the city were using sorcery to hinder the upcoming meetings. Such practices are not uncommon in places like Africa. Many people turn to witchcraft to find answers to their problems or in expectation of physical healing for their ailments. Witches also are known to put curses on people and other things that they or the person paying them sees fit. Upon hearing this news, I reminded myself to simply move forward by faith, knowing God will get the glory no matter what.

I had a direct flight from Newark, New Jersey, in the U.S. to Accra, Ghana. Because it was such a long, non-stop flight, I chose to pay a little extra for my seat. This would give me just a little more leg room. I was one of the first ones on the plane and headed toward my seat. When I got to my seat, I noticed it was two rows *behind* the seats with the extra leg room. I checked my receipt to make sure I had indeed purchased the better seat, and I had. I told the nearest flight attendant this was not the seat I purchased. It was the right seat number, but it did not provide the extra leg room. She told me I would have to talk to a gate agent about my seat situation. Hearing this, I was frustrated. International flights are usually full, and now I found myself having to maneuver my way back against the flow of oncoming passengers. I finally made it back to the gate agents.

God Uses Chaos To Move Us

The man at the gate was very busy boarding the other passengers, and I was an obvious nuisance to him. I explained my situation and showed him my receipt. Fortunately, he found me another seat on the plane that was satisfactory to me. Finally, I made it to my new seat, relieved the ordeal was resolved. It was not the seat for which I paid, but, quite honestly, it was better. I thought to myself, "Thank you, Lord. That little bit of disruption, though it was annoying, was worth it for a better seat." And yes, it was the Lord's doing.

A few minutes after takeoff, the man sitting next to me asked, "So where are you headed in Ghana?"

"Obuasi," I simply replied.

He then asked, "What is your reason for going to Obuasi?"

I told him I am a minister and would be ministering all week in the city.

The man looked at me and said, "I have a radio station in Obuasi. I will arrange it so that you can have free airtime to talk about your program in the city."

I was stunned. In a minor moment of disorder with something as petty as an airline seat, God was there the whole time, orchestrating His purpose and His plan. I was going to get free airtime!

Once I arrived in the city, I was greeted by the pastor and his team, none of whom I had ever met in person. I shared with them how we were going to get free airtime to advertise this ministry event in their city. The pastor was surprised to hear my story and told me how quality airtime was very expensive. The radio station contacted me the next day and proceeded to do exactly what the man next to me on the plane said he would do. For the first three days, I preached to an entire city on the radio. There is no way I, the pastor, or anyone else could have made this happen. But God was in the confusion of a minor situation bringing forth His purpose.

God is not only the God of the big picture of our lives, but He is also the God of the smallest details in our lives. Even in those seemingly unimportant, irritating, and confusing moments of our lives, He is there. He has a plan that is being unfolded for His glory. We must learn to try to find Him even in the little things.

When I think back on how annoyed I had been because of my seat situation, I have to laugh. Little did I know that God was up to something of much greater importance. This story was just the beginning of my journey to Ghana. Over the next few days, God would demonstrate His greatness in the chaos in even more remarkable ways.

CHAPTER 11

A Sign for a Housekeeper

"For in the day of trouble
he will keep me safe in his dwelling."

PSALM 27:5 NIV

God Is Watching Over And Protecting Us

When I first arrived in the city of Obuasi, I was taken
to one of the city's nicer hotels where I would be staying. I
checked into my room and started to unpack. The pastor
returned a short while later to take me to a prayer meeting
at his church. When I returned to my hotel room, I noticed a
slight dripping coming from the room's small air conditioner.
Water had started to accumulate, and some of my things were
in jeopardy of getting wet. I called the front desk and they
sent maintenance people to look at it. Upon examining the
air conditioner, they said they would fix it later and offered
me the option of changing rooms. Like the change of seats on
the plane, changing rooms was a logical decision, but it was
an annoyance. I decided to change rooms, packed up all my

belongings, and proceeded to a room across the hall. I settled in, looking forward to the days ahead.

The next day, one of the staff members from housekeeping introduced herself to me. She was a very kind lady who was responsible for cleaning many rooms, including mine. She said she would clean my room every day that I was there. She knew I was a Christian minister, and, during one of our brief conversations, I discovered she was a Muslim. I could tell she enjoyed our conversations and was interested in what I had to say. At first, she equated the God of the Christian and Muslim faiths. At this, I was quick to convey the truth to her. The two are not the same. They are completely different.

To help her understand, I told her about the love of Jesus and the power of forgiveness. A God of love and forgiveness is a foreign concept to most Muslims. The idea that there is a God that not only loves them but also forgives is not rational to the Muslim mind. Sensing the lack of peace in her own faith and seeing the joyless pain in her eyes, I took a couple of minutes to share the gospel message that cuts to the heart of many unbelievers. I did not overwhelm her but had a short conversation about a God who loves her.

God Is In The Chaos Not Wanting Any To Perish

I told her how He sent His son, Jesus Christ, to die on a cross so that all who put their trust in Him could be forgiven. I could tell the Lord was moving on her and that she wanted to know more, but it was not safe. She was a Muslim, and I was a Christian. If the wrong people found out about our conversations, it could have been dangerous for either or both of us.

There is a significant population of Muslims in Obuasi. During my stay in Ghana, a missionary was killed by Muslims not far from where I was staying. It is extremely dangerous for any Muslim who accepts Christ. He or she could suffer immediate persecution, even from a spouse. In most instances, they are rejected—sometimes even killed—by their own families. It is equally dangerous for the Christian who talks to a Muslim about the saving grace of Jesus. Nevertheless, we are still called to go and reach them.

A few days later, I woke up from a restful sleep to what sounded like large vacuums. It was quite loud. I was extremely tired, and my body was still adjusting from the jet leg and time change caused by traveling from the U.S. I hadn't been asleep very long and it was still very early in the morning. I remember thinking, *What kind of a hotel cleans with heavy equipment this early in the morning?*

I tried and tried and tried to fall asleep again, but it was useless. The noise continued through the early morning and went on for a few hours. I might have drifted off a couple of times for short periods, but I did not get much sleep that night.

He Is The God Of Miracles

Realizing the futility of trying to sleep, I decided to get up and begin my day. I was frustrated and very annoyed that the hotel allowed their people to work when their guests undoubtedly were sleeping. Usually, when things like this occur overseas, I pause and remind myself that I'm in another country and try to find the humor in the situation.

I had a long day ahead of me and I was already exhausted. About the time I completed my morning routine, someone suddenly knocked on my door. It was still early enough that I wondered who would be knocking on my door at this time of the morning. When I opened the door, standing in the hall was the Muslim lady from housekeeping. I couldn't help but notice the equipment in the long hallway and quickly concluded that's what I had been hearing all night long. The woman asked me if I had water all over my room. I was a bit confused and replied, "No, I don't have water all over my room." I opened the door more fully for her to look in and see. As she looked in my room, she was shocked at what she didn't see—water all over my room. She stared at my room in disbelief, completely confused. At this point, I wondered what was going on. I had no idea why she was so perplexed.

Several hours ago, she began to explain, water flooded into the hotel leaving every room and hallway twelve inches deep in water. "Every room but yours!" she said, adding, "We have been out here sucking up water out of the hallway and all the rooms for many hours." I looked out in the hallway and it was still wet. There was a brown water stain on the walls that was nearly a foot high in some places. She looked at me like I was someone special. I looked back at her and told her this was a sign for her that Jesus is real and that He loves her.

The employees of the hotel couldn't make sense of this incident. My room was in the middle of the hallway, dry as could be, and yet every other room on the floor had flooded. Every door, including mine, had separation between the door and the floor, yet no water seeped into my room. I walked around the hotel and took pictures of the aftermath of the flooding. There were water marks on all the walls in the hall and in all the rooms except mine. There were water marks on all the furniture in every room except mine. After I closed the door, I was astonished by this miracle. I remembered that a few days before, I had been assigned to a different room. Because of an annoying water drip from the air conditioner, I moved. While it was inconvenient to move to a new room, God had a plan not only to protect my belongings, but He was also going to demonstrate His greatness to a Muslim lady through a miracle.

God dealt with the chaos before I was even aware that chaos was coming my way. Initially, having to change rooms was an aggravation I would have preferred to avoid. I never could have imagined how significant it was. In retrospect, the changing of rooms was momentous. As people of faith, we must realize that God is always watching over and protecting us, even when we are not aware of the chaos headed our way. He is there, moving on our behalf, demonstrating His awesome love not only to His children but also to those who have not yet come to know our loving and forgiving Father.

CHAPTER 12

Darkness Defeated

*"For he has rescued us from
the dominion of darkness and
brought us into the kingdom
of the Son he loves."*

COLOSSIANS 1:13 NIV

God Demonstrates His Greatness In The Darkness

I had the privilege of meeting a Nigerian bishop the second day I ministered to the church in Obuasi. The bishop was a friend of the pastor and wanted to come to the special meetings. That night in the service, the bishop witnessed something he had never seen before. It was a service of powerful deliverance. He and the others in attendance had seen deliverances take place many times, but not like this night. To the bishop, this deliverance service was different.

The next day, the bishop inquired about what had taken place the previous night. He said he had performed deliverances many times in the past but, after many years, had gotten discouraged and stopped performing them. The reason, he explained, was because he had noticed the demons kept coming back to those people he thought had been set free. This was not the first time I had heard about preachers being discouraged and discontinuing deliverance services for the same reason. I took a few minutes to explain some concepts about deliverance to encourage the bishop. As we talked, I could see he was inspired and wanted to learn more.

In the afternoon of the fourth day, the pastor and I headed to the radio station just as we had the previous days. However, on this day, the bishop joined us, eager to participate in the radio program. As usual, the pastor began the program by talking about what was happening in the services. He encouraged people to come to the meetings. When he finished, I was given time to minister and was followed by the bishop, who wanted to share a few words with the audience.

True Faith Has Power Over The Darkness

The bishop prophesied about what was going to happen in that evening's service. He declared that many of the people were going to be delivered and set free from demonic powers. He was so intense I couldn't help but think, *Oh my! Lord, do you hear what the bishop is saying?* I wondered who was preaching that evening. I was stunned by the bishop's powerful words. That evening, as I got ready for the service, I thought about what was said at the radio station. I submitted all of it to the Lord, trusting that He is capable of doing great things. I was ready to go at the time I was told my ride would be there. I was looking forward to this service. God had already done some great things, and I could feel the momentum building.

Waiting for my ride to come, I paced back and forth in my hotel room. I was like an athlete getting ready for the big game. I kept looking at the time and noticed that my ride was thirty minutes late. *No big deal*, I thought to myself. *Things happen and I'm sure they will be here any second.* I continued to pace, occasionally going over to the window to see if anyone had pulled up. They were an hour late and still no ride. About this time, I started to get a little aggravated with the situation. I was supposed to be the guest speaker, the service had started, I was not even on my way to the church, and nobody had called to tell me what the holdup was. I was getting very upset. As I waited, I reflected on what was said at the radio station about this evening's service. I considered how amazing it was going to be, and how God was going to show up in a big way. Many lives would be delivered from all kinds of bondages. But where was my ride? Soon, the hour turned into an hour and a half and then two hours. Still no ride, still no communication! I was perplexed and wondered what was happening. My aggravation now started to turn to anger. Who does this? I understand that things can happen, but they should at least communicate with me! The service was supposed to start at 6:30 p.m. It was now 9:00 p.m. and still no word. I was beyond upset. "That's it!" I said to myself. "I'm taking off my suit that I have been pacing in for hours and I am going to bed! If for some reason they show up, I'm not going! This is chaos!"

Just then there was a knock at my door. I took a deep breath, trying to pull myself together. I answered the door and, sure enough, it was my ride. The driver looked at me and said,

"Pastor, we have a big problem." Looking at him as kindly as I could, I asked, "What is the problem?" He told me the city's electric power had gone out a few hours ago. He said the people at the church had been waiting for me for the past two hours.

"Is this normal?" I asked him.

"No, not like this, this is not normal," he replied.

The entire city was in the dark. When I learned of the blackout, I considered what had been prophesied earlier in the day about the evening service. It didn't take long to connect the blackout to the prophetic word and realize that what was taking place was spiritual warfare.

I recalled that even before I left for Ghana, I had heard witchcraft was being performed to hinder what God wanted to do. And what God wanted to do was deliver many people from demonic powers and bondages. This kind of spiritual confrontation is not all that uncommon in places like Africa. I looked at my driver and said, "Let's pray." I said a simple prayer and took authority over this situation in the name of Jesus. By this time, my anger and frustration had subsided, and I was in a place of peace knowing that God was in control of the chaos.

God's Light Is Victorious In The Darkness

We headed back to the church. The appearance of the city as we approached it was unnerving. It was pitch black. Demonic powers had invaded Obuasi to destroy what God had purposed for this night's service. I was dumbfounded at what I saw. We finally made it to the church. It was filled with people. I stood in awe of the patience exhibited by all these people; they had waited patiently for hours in the darkness. But they had come hungry for a breakthrough in their lives and would not be discouraged. Realizing this, I humbly put my trust in Jesus before I got out of the car. As soon as I stepped out of the car, all the electricity came back on. The people rejoiced, and the pastor quickly started the service. That night, the Holy Spirit touched many people.

God's presence was real and evident. Many experienced healing or were set free from demons. Demonic kingdoms fled the scene. While people had waited patiently for their breakthrough, light had come into the darkness. In all the confusion, God was there. All along, the Lord knew what He wanted to accomplish—to demonstrate His greatness in the darkness.

CHAPTER 13

Catalyst

"The Spirit of the Lord God is upon Me,
Because the Lord has anointed Me
To preach good tidings to the poor;
He has sent Me to heal the brokenhearted,
To proclaim liberty to the captives,
And the opening of the prison
to those who are bound."

ISAIAH 61:1 NKJV

Sometimes God Allows Chaos To Serve As A Catalyst

I have always had a desire to go to other nations of the world to preach the Gospel. After all, the very fabric of the great commission is "to go." The day came that the Lord provided an opportunity for me to travel to Ukraine for an international conference. Church leaders from Eastern Europe and Northern Asia were coming to learn more about the supernatural power of God. I was going by faith, not knowing what to expect. I would merely be one of hundreds in attendance. I had a desire to learn from whoever would be speaking. I just felt like I was supposed to go, so I went.

Once I arrived, it didn't take long before I realized the Lord had set me up. He had other plans for my being there. I arrived on a Saturday and the conference was not scheduled to start until Monday morning. The host pastor, who did not know me and whom I had never met, said that I would be preaching at his church the following morning. I only knew about this pastor through a couple of my American friends who were ministers. But being scheduled to preach without any advance knowledge was fine with me, and I looked forward to the opportunity.

The next morning, I preached a simple gospel message of hope. After the service, the pastor pulled me aside and told me the keynote speakers were going to be delayed for a couple of days. He then asked me to speak at the conference for the first two days. I was very honored and, of course, agreed to help in any way I could. I arrived at the conference ready to teach the following morning. The room was filled with Christian leaders from many countries who were hungry to learn from God's word. It wasn't long before I noticed a big video camera in the center of the main auditorium. I inquired about it and learned they were video recording the entire conference. This was very unnerving for me. I had never spoken at an international conference or had used a Russian-speaking interpreter.

Learn To Expect The Unexpected

When I signed up for this conference, I expected to come to learn and observe. I knew in my heart I was supposed to be here. Now, because of some unforeseen circumstances, I was being thrust out to preach in an international setting in front of hundreds of church leaders while being video recorded. I was nervous when it was time for me to speak. The only introduction they could give me was that I am a pastor from the United States. I walked up to the microphone with my interpreter.

I knew that one of the focuses of the conference was the supernatural power of God. So, I began to speak what the Lord laid on my heart. Things quickly appeared to be going well. The audience was great. Their desire to learn was obvious as they took notes as fast as they could write. Then it happened. About halfway through a teaching session, a man in the back of the auditorium suddenly began to convulse. It was obvious to all that this man was having a serious problem. It wasn't long before I realized what was happening. The man was manifesting a demon out in the open for all to see.

I did not stop teaching but pressed on. I noticed a handful of people had gathered around the man, trying to deal with the situation as best as they could. I continued the lesson, believing the people in the back were fully capable of taking care of the situation. I tried to keep my composure and kept pressing on with the teaching. After a few minutes of this awkward commotion (or should I say, "CHAOS!"), one of the ladies helping in the back looked up at me and shouted in Russian, "Help him! Aren't you going to help him?!"

Only Jesus Can Set The Captive Free

Immediately all eyes were turned towards me. I just happened to be the guy that was teaching about the supernatural, and now everyone there wanted to see this man get set free from this demon. Forget we are in the middle of a teaching session, not to mention the session was being video recorded. Everyone there wanted to see what I would do next. Stunned at what was taking place, I stopped teaching and said, "Bring him up to the front." It took a few people to help the man to the front of the stage.

While they were bringing him, I thought to myself, *What am I doing? They are bringing a man to me that is manifesting a demon, and they want me to drive it out right now in front of a large audience with video cameras recording! This is crazy!* Then I started thinking, *What if I can't help him right now? What if I am made to look like a fool? They are looking to me, the person who is teaching about being used by God to set the captive free, to set this man free from this demon.*

It wasn't as if I had never participated in deliverances. In fact, I'd been involved in many of them. Most were done behind closed doors in private meetings. I'd even done several mass deliverances in crowds, but not like this. This was different. This was one man filled with a demon, a massive audience scrutinizing every little thing I'd do, and a video camera recording it. In a moment, as they were bringing this man up to me for ministry, I turned around with my back to the audience, and said a simple, desperate prayer: "Jesus, help me!"

As soon as I said these words, a spirit of faith came upon me that I had felt many times in the past. I turned around and there stood this demon-possessed man. He could barely stay on his feet. His body was convulsing, and he was in and out of consciousness. Quickly, I took authority over the spirit and commanded it to go down in Jesus's name. The demon did exactly as I said. At that point, the man came back to full consciousness. I asked him some questions and then led him in a prayer. Speaking again to the demon, I commanded it to come up. It came up quickly, and it was not happy. It glared at me, trying its hardest to cause me to fear it.

I have seen this same glare many times in the past. I knew this demon's power had been broken and his right to stay in this man had been revoked. At this point, I commanded the evil spirit to leave in the name of Jesus. The demon left, and the man came back to himself—free and in his right mind. The man's countenance changed immediately. Everyone in the auditorium that day witnessed the supernatural power of God. The people in the audience began to rejoice over what they had just witnessed—the power of Jesus defeating the forces of darkness.

Believe me, I was also overjoyed and thankful. In the midst of the chaos, God did not let me down. All I had to do was move forward in faith trusting in His might. God allowed this situation to happen. This one deliverance was just the beginning. Every day, God confirmed His word. By the end of the conference, many people were set free and we had miracles occur daily.

When I look back at that day, I see God's hand in it all. He was there waiting and longing to set people free. For that to happen, God had to allow a little chaos to serve as a catalyst. It all began with chaos, but in the chaos God is!

CHAPTER 14

Master Class

"Fear not, for I am with you;
Be not dismayed, for I am your God.
I will strengthen you, Yes, I will help you,
I will uphold you with My righteous right hand."

ISAIAH 41:10 NKJV

Sometimes Chaos Is Part Of God's Plan

Shortly after that morning session ended, the pastor overseeing the international conference pulled me aside and informed me I would be holding Master Class at 3:00 p.m. Although I had no idea what Master Class was, I agreed to do it.

I asked him, "What is Master Class?"

"Master Class," he said, "is when you will be on the stage, and we will bring people up to you who have demons. You will drive them out in front of the church leaders, so they can learn how to do it." *WHAT?*

I had presumed Master Class to be a special teaching in the area of healing and deliverance. Everything in me wanted to tell this pastor, "That's crazy!" I never heard of anything like this. Public deliverances—one right after another—while people took notes? There is no telling what can happen when casting a demon out of someone. Things can get crazy fast. And to do it like a production line in front of a live audience with video cameras recording everything just seemed absurd. I had gotten myself into a "You have got to be kidding me" situation. I had two hours to mentally process what was going to take place. As bizarre as this activity sounded, I showed up at 3:00 p.m. to teach "Master Class." The building was full, and I could sense the excitement and anticipation as to what everyone was hoping to witness and learn.

Over the past couple of hours, I had wondered who would be willing to go through a public deliverance like this. Talk about exposing your dirty laundry for everyone to see! As I came into the room, I looked to the left side of the stage where there was a row of chairs filled with broken-spirited people. They did not seem to care about anything other than getting their miracle. They didn't care that people were going to be watching or that everything would be recorded by video. Nobody was forcing them to be there. They were hurting people filled with the hope that Jesus was going to set them free. My heart moved with compassion for them.

God Longs For Us To Cry Out To Him

Finally, the time had come to start Master Class. I walked up on the stage with my interpreter. With every step I took, I prayed, for I was extremely nervous. Hundreds of eyes were watching me. They seemed to be smiling. I glanced at the video camera that was practically right on top of me and thought, *How in the world did I get in this situation!*

I gulped and looked over at all the people longing to come up to be delivered. I prayed and invited the first person in line to join us on the stage. As she approached the stage, my heart cried out, "Jesus, please help me! Please show up! I need you NOW! Please help these hurting people and please don't let me look like a fool!" Knowing I had to quickly make a shift from harboring feelings of anxiety to exercising my faith, I chose to trust the Lord. He was the reason I was standing on the stage. "Lord, do what you want," I said to myself. "If I look like a fool, so be it. Let's go!"

The woman, now standing before me, suddenly began to manifest a demon. It came up snarling and contorting. The eyes turned dark and sinister. Most of the time, I like to get information from a person before I begin ministering to them. But sometimes you have to go backwards.

"What is your name, spirit?" I commanded (I had to do this through my interpreter). The demon just stared at me, pure evil pouring out of the eyes. "What is your name?" I persisted. This went on for a few minutes, after which I determined I wasn't going to get any cooperation from the demon. Knowing that all eyes were on me, I tried another tactic. I leaned towards the woman and whispered in her ear, "You evil spirit, you will stop your works now and do what I command in Jesus's name."

Right then, I heard people in the audience trying to tell me something. I couldn't understand anything they were saying. I glanced at my interpreter, and she said to me, "They are saying she can't hear."

"Great," I said to myself. "Not only do I have a demonized woman in front of me, she also can't hear!"

In the craziness of the moment, however, that information was helpful to me. I put my hands over her ears and commanded the deaf spirit to release her and for her to be healed in the name of Jesus. The demon then started to talk through the woman. It gave up its name. Sensing all its powers over this woman had been broken, I ordered the demon to leave in the name of Jesus. It left quickly. The lady came back to herself, a look of shock and joy on her face. "I can hear, I can hear!" she cried out. At this, all the people in the audience shouted and clapped, praising God for the wonderful miracle they had just witnessed.

The others waiting in line kept coming, one after another. Many of them had demons. Others simply needed healing. When Master Class was over, my heart was overjoyed with how good the Lord is. Healings and deliverances continued throughout the conference. Miracles took place every day and God confirmed His word with signs and wonders.

Learn To Find God When You Need His Help

Honestly, I still think Master Class is crazy, but the fruit has been remarkable. In addition to people being delivered and/or healed, many church leaders learned how to heal the brokenhearted and set the captive free. Since that conference, I have been invited back to this same region many times. And yes, I have participated in many more Master Classes. Each time, before I begin, I pray under my breath, "Please, Jesus, help me!" And every time He does.

I am thankful the Lord allows us to find Him in our time of need, in those moments when we feel the situation is bigger than we are. God longs for us to cry out to Him so that He can allow His greatness to manifest in our chaos.

CHAPTER 15

Don't Worry. Jesus is with Us

"You will keep him in perfect peace,
whose mind is stayed on You,
because he trusts in You."

ISAIAH 26:3 NKJV

God Brings Light Into Darkness

In 2014, war broke out in Ukraine. I was scheduled to go back to Ukraine—specifically Eastern Ukraine—where the war was being fought. I'd been to this region before and the people there hold a special place in my heart. When I arrived, my host provided me with the agenda as to the times and places I would be ministering. On this particular trip, I would spend the first part of the week ministering to hundreds of Bible college students just outside the war zone.

I could sense the atmosphere was different from my previous trips. Many of the students had family, friends, or both in the war zone. Some were already ministering in those areas and would be returning to the chaos in a few days. No one had any idea how long this war might last. Nonetheless, these students continued to pursue the Lord and trust Him to use their lives regardless of what tomorrow held.

I taught at the Bible college for three days. On the fourth day, we were informed that two Russian Separatists had sat in on one of the services. They wore video spy glasses and recorded everything that took place. The school's security team discovered them and had them arrested. The Russian Separatists had heard that Americans would be speaking and sent spies into the meeting to learn what was taking place there. Obviously, they were very paranoid and thought we might be propagating something that could hinder their cause. It became a big local news story given all that was happening in the region.

After ministering at the school, they decided to have me visit some of their churches in the war zone. The name of the region is Donetsk. This is a key city that the Russian Separatists had already captured. As usual, I did as they asked and trusted God. When I arrived, I was told not to speak any English in public for safety reasons. As we drove into the city, we passed a government building that had been taken over by the Russian Separatists. Armed soldiers stood in front of the building. Nearby, a sign, written in English, issued a warning: "Americans get out!"

Christ In Us Is The Victory

It was at this point that I really began to understand how dangerous this area was for me. Across the street from the government building was another large building. The lead pastor, whose name is Alexander, looked at me and told me this is where I would be preaching the next day. That evening, they took me to another place in Donetsk to minister. As always, God showed up, and we had a glorious time in that meeting. After the service, Alexander took me and a few other men from the church out for a quick meal. We got out of the car and walked into the restaurant. I'd been sitting down for a minute when Pastor Alexander suddenly came over to my interpreter. The expression on his face was one of great concern. My interpreter turned to me and said, "Hurry! We must go now!" I got up quickly and headed toward the door. The interpreter, walking alongside of me, explained what was happening. A Russian Separatist in the restaurant had heard me speaking English and knew I was an American. He had made a call to alert others about my being there. He told them he would keep an eye on me until backup came. Clearly, I was in great danger!

It was about this time that people began to be taken captive in the region. Soldiers, reporters, ministers, and others who the Separatists deemed a threat were being arrested and held against their will. There were many stories of people disappearing and even being killed. Furthermore, the persecution of Christian believers was increasing. My friends hurried me into the car and we sped away. The driver drove extremely fast through the city, making many turns in hopes of losing those who might be following us. It was at that moment that it hit me. Our lives were in real danger. Feelings came over me like I never before experienced. This was a real, physical threat to my life. *What would happen if these men caught us?* I wondered. Fear gripped my heart. I thought about my wife and children. In a matter of seconds, I went from feeling safe to fearing for my life. It all seemed surreal. Only a short while ago, we had left a great service where God visited us in a mighty way. I felt safe. Now, we were fleeing for our lives. When my interpreter noticed my countenance, he looked at me, smiled, and said, "Don't worry, Jesus is with us!" Those words brought a smile to my face. Deep down, I knew he was right. In dwelling on my own fear, it was the jolt I needed. And in that moment, I made a shift in my spirit, and put my trust in the Lord.

Today, I laugh at that incident, even as serious and potentially dangerous as it was. When something like that happens, what are you going to do? When you're in the chaos, you're in the chaos! We can't allow fear to overcome us. When it hits us, we must make a shift in our thinking and choose to lean upon the God of peace.

The next night, I preached across the street from the government building now controlled by the Separatists. Boldness came over me when I started to preach, and I noticed people from the church getting up to close the windows. I knew they were trying to protect me and didn't want anyone outside to hear me speaking English.

True Faith Finds Peace In The Lord

That night, God moved in the service and many people received healing and deliverance. Outside the walls of the church, all throughout the region, a war was raging daily. Yet, in all of this, we found God in the chaos. He brought His light into the darkness.

As believers in Christ, we must always remember our spiritual enemy will come along and try to distract us from the peace that comes from God. Even though our circumstances may be unsettling at times, we should remind ourselves of the promise found in Isaiah: "You will keep him in perfect peace, whose mind is stayed on You, because he trusts in You" (Isaiah 26:3 NKJV).

CHAPTER 16

Troubles in this World

*"I have told you these things,
so that in me you may have peace.
In this world you will have trouble.
But take heart! I have overcome the world."*

JOHN 16:33 NIV

The Life Of A Believer Is Not Always Pleasant

Jesus spoke these words in conclusion to all the things He taught His disciples following the Last Supper. He knew how badly their lives would be shaken when He, their Messiah, would be unjustly arrested, humiliated, beaten, and nailed to a cross. Chaos would challenge everything the disciples hoped and believed, even though Jesus tried to prepare them for it. Anticipating this, and also the persecution to come, Jesus looked to put their minds at ease with these words of comfort. Jesus told His disciples—and us—that choosing to live our lives for Him would be troublesome and, at times, chaotic. Finding

God in chaos begins with a realization that Jesus declared, "In Me you may have peace."

Trouble is inevitable. Persecution is sure. But in Christ, there is peace. If you are just of this world, it is impossible to have peace when chaos surrounds you. If you are in Him, He is in you. As such, you can have peace even when you see nothing but trouble coming your way. Why? Because, Jesus has overcome the world. That's why.

When Jesus spoke these words of encouragement to His disciples, He was prophesying a future reality, knowing that He still had to endure—through the cross—death and the grave. But He knew He would overcome both by rising again on the third day. In Christ, we already have the victory even though we must endure hardships. We can be victorious through the chaos. Jesus is the guarantee of our future reality.

Shortly after I left to go back home to the U.S., the situation in Ukraine intensified. There was a great deal the media was not reporting regarding the war. Much of it had to do with the persecution of the Christians in the war zone, particularly the Protestant churches. My friends there were (and still are) a part of a big movement of nearly 400 churches in that region of the world. The only denomination not being persecuted was the Orthodox Church. The reason is simple: they are easily controlled by government leadership.

God's People Demonstrate Courage In Chaos

The Protestants, especially those who carry a true Biblical worldview, pose a genuine threat to the mindset of the government agenda being propagated. Shortly after I returned home, more Protestant pastors began to disappear. The Separatists felt if they could restrict the leadership, it would cause the churches to dissipate. My friend, Pastor Alexander, along with other men of God, had a bounty put on his life. One day, Alexander sent me a message: "Mike, can you believe it? There is a bounty on my head for lots of money." Naturally, for safety reasons, he had to sneak his wife and three little children out of the city. Others from the church stayed in hopes of advancing the gospel.

A few months later I went back to Ukraine. I learned that many of the church leaders had been forced out of the area seized by the Separatists. Some had paid the ultimate sacrifice—their lives. I had the opportunity to spend time with several of the persecuted believers and the privilege to hear their stories of real faith in the face of trouble. The courage these men and women possessed was invigorating.

While I was there, in an area just outside the war zone, Alexander got an alarming phone call. It was about one of his church leaders who had continued to serve in the war zone despite knowing the risks of persecution and possible death. He had just been abducted by the Separatists. When Pastor Alexander told me who it was, my heart ached upon hearing it was a young preacher I had worked with on my previous trip. This was not someone I had read about in a book or other media outlets; it was someone I knew and with whom I had spent time. He was the leader from the first service I had in Donetsk only a couple months before.

The Separatists had pulled up and forced him into a van. They placed a tire around the young man's body and then tied him to a tree. The Separatists beat him severely. They burned him with cigarettes all over his bleeding body. He suffered all this simply because he was a church leader trying to help the hurting people in his city. Despite his beating, he did not break. God empowered him to stand in his time of trouble and chaos. A couple of days later the young minister was found alive and taken to safety. He was fortunate to make it out alive.

God's People Can Find Peace In Their Suffering

It is extremely humbling to hear how persecuted believers endured such hatred. The persecution of Christians is rapidly increasing. All over the world, believers are warring against the Antichrist spirit that is out to defeat the advancement of God's kingdom. In my ministry travels, I have had many encounters with this sad reality. To escape capture, some of my friends have had to flee from their homes, leaving everything behind but the clothes on their backs. Some have been unjustly arrested, beaten, and even shot at with guns. Many have stories of how their friends have been brutally killed just because they were Christians.

While on a trip to India, a pastor approached me for prayer. He told me how a couple of years before, he went into a village to share the gospel message. A gang of men met him, beat him severely, and left him for dead, again, because he was preaching about Jesus. He had made it out alive, but the beating left him nearly crippled. Severe problems with his spine made it almost unbearable for him to walk. He said no doctor had been able to help him, and he asked me to pray for him. With a simple prayer of faith, God supernaturally healed him. But his story is like so many others who have endured great affliction to advance the gospel of Jesus Christ.

The life of a true believer is not always pleasant. In fact, it's often quite the contrary; it's a life of reckless abandonment for the cause of Christ. Yes, they know that in this world they will have trouble. Yes, they know suffering will come. But true believers do not live for this world. When they say "Yes" to Christ, they are transformed into another kingdom. They now live to please their King. They press on in the chaos. They learn to find peace in their suffering. They know that Jesus Himself conquered death, hell, and the grave and through Him, they too shall overcome.

CHAPTER 17

The Midnight Hour

"But at midnight Paul and Silas were praying
and singing hymns to God,
and the prisoners were listening to them.
Suddenly there was a great earthquake,
so that the foundations of the prison were shaken;
and immediately all the doors were opened,
and everyone's chains were loosed."

ACTS 16:25-26 NKJV

God Can Do Wonders In Your Midnight Hour

In Acts 16, as Paul and Silas were on their way to pray, a young woman began to follow them. The woman, a slave who had a spirit of divination, had made her owners a great deal of money by fortune telling. For days, she had shadowed Paul and Silas, crying out who they were. Greatly annoyed, Paul finally turned to the woman and commanded the spirit to leave her. When the woman's owners saw that they would not be able to make money off her anymore, they were furious. Paul and Silas were dragged to the authorities and accused of causing trouble and teaching things not in accordance with Roman law. Their clothes were ripped off and they were severely beaten. After this horrible beating, they were thrown into prison and their feet fastened in stocks. It is interesting to note this incident occurred around midnight. Things had quieted down, and the jailer was sleeping. Paul and Silas were probably in too much pain and discomfort to fall asleep. They had plenty of time to reflect on the day's events.

It is at this time—the midnight hour—when things have quieted down, and you have time to dwell on your chaotic situation that the enemy, the devil, comes to torment you. He tries to fill you with fear and wants you to blame God for the troubles you are experiencing.

God's People Still Worship In Their Suffering

At this point, many people break and lose faith. They can't find God in their situation. These two men had every reason to complain about their situation. They had done nothing wrong—they were merely on their way to pray when the trouble started. The sad truth is that many of us get angry that God allows us to experience such torment solely because we love Him enough to do what He asked us to do.

Paul and Silas now found themselves in a chaotic situation. Imagine how they must have felt. It would have been easy for them to be confused or bitter that God allowed this to happen. It would have been natural for them to be overcome with fear because of what might happen next. All hell seemed to be coming against them, yet did their faith crumble? Not at all; in fact, just the opposite happened. Instead of giving up on God and giving in to the fear of the moment, they began to call out to God in their chaos. How? They started to pray and worship in a dark, damp dungeon. With their torn and bloodied bodies still throbbing, they sought God in their suffering. The Lord then responded to Paul and Silas's faithfulness by sending an earthquake that opened all the cell doors and loosened the prisoners' chains.

I was scheduled to preach at a wonderful church in Ukraine. I had been to this church many times. Upon my arrival, I was told that Bishop Dmitry, the pastor, was not going to be there. Naturally, I was curious as to why. I had not seen him for some time and I was looking forward to meeting with him again. One of the church leaders proceeded to tell me that, three weeks before my arrival, the bishop was beaten up by soldiers in the war zone. Hearing of his persecution became another surreal moment for me, and I felt humbled knowing I was to preach two services the next day in his church. The following day, after ministering, I connected with another church leader who explained in greater detail what had happened to Bishop Dmitry.

The bishop and three other church leaders were on their way into the war zone to check on the new churches that were forming there. When driving into the war zone, you must go through many military roadblocks. You pray nothing out of the ordinary happens. It can be unnerving at times, as I know from my own experiences of going through many of them. Once you get to the war zone, you'll find two types of soldiers: ones that ignore your presence and the others that despise you being there. An anti-Christian culture is developing everywhere around the world, and Ukraine is no different.

The bishop and his companions had been to this same area a few times prior, and some of the soldiers began to threaten them. They did not want any Christian preachers in that region anymore. Nevertheless, knowing this, my friends still felt compelled to bring the light of the gospel to those suffering in the war-torn cities. On this particular day, the team had finished ministering and set off on their journey back to the safe zone. As they drove away, they were stopped by soldiers, who forcefully removed Dmitry from his car and commenced to beating him. They dragged him around the corner and out of sight from his friends who were still in the car.

God Delights In Helping His People

Bishop Dmitry looked at the men who were beating him and said, "You carry those guns, but I have Jesus." The soldiers, ignoring him, did not let up and continued to beat him. They hoped this thrashing would discourage the bishop and others like him from bringing the message of Jesus to the people in that area. Those who remained in the car didn't know what to do. Fear held them in its grip as they could only guess what was happening to the bishop. They knew of other church leaders that had been tortured, and some even murdered. They wondered if this was the end for the bishop and if they would be next. Terror paralyzed two of the passengers in the car to the extent they were unable to even pray. But the other person in the car began to cry out to the Lord. Her faith overwhelmed her fear. Within a couple of minutes of intense praying, suddenly, out of nowhere, hail began to fall from the sky. The hail was so violent the soldiers stopped beating Bishop Dmitry and ran for cover. The bishop stumbled back to the car and, as soon as he got in, they quickly sped away and made it back to the safe zone. The person who cried out to the Lord, a woman, is a friend of mine. She told me she prayed so hard, with such passion, it was as if she had left her body. And in a mighty demonstration of His power and love, the Lord answered her faithful reaction to the chaos that threatened them that evening. In the chaos... in their time of need...she found God, and God delivered them.

Like Paul and Silas, we can find ourselves in a dreadful situation, our faith tested to the brink. If you feel you have done everything right, but you are still feeling defeated...if your faith has been weakened and you are surrounded by darkness... remember that it is never too late to cry out. God can do wonders in your "midnight hour."

CHAPTER 18

Fire Beetle Christians

*"But you shall receive power when the Holy Spirit
has come upon you; and you shall be witnesses to
Me in Jerusalem, and in all Judea and Samaria,
and to the end of the earth."*

ACTS 1:8 NKJV

God's Kingdom Thrives In Chaos

Fire beetles are unique insects that thrive in fire-scorched areas. When forest fires break out, all creatures are forced out to pursue safety and self-preservation. Fire beetles do the complete opposite. They are drawn to the fires. In fact, the fire beetles were strategically created with sensors that can detect forest fires miles away. These sensors direct the beetles to the fire. While all the other creatures are running from the fire, these beetles head for the flames. They were equipped to thrive in the fire-scorched forest. It is the ideal place for them to lay their eggs safely and multiply in numbers. It is a safe place because all their predators have been driven out by the fire.

On the day of Pentecost, a fire was ignited in the life of the early church. This fire changed the lives of Jesus's disciples and other believers. They were changed into men and women who were willing to pursue lost souls at any cost. They went into areas where there was great persecution. Their faith enabled them to run into the fires of trouble and danger to advance the kingdom of God. Despite persecution, the early church rapidly multiplied. They were like fire beetles thriving in the fires of chaos and tribulation.

In my travels, I have met many Christian "fire beetles." They are men and women who, not living for this world, seek the chaos, darkness, and confusion when all others are fleeing. In the war zones of Ukraine, many of the Protestant ministries have been pushed out. There are places where there are no Christians at all. The group I was with had started sending teams of people into the war-torn cities to aid the people and to try to establish churches. They would take as much food as possible to feed those who were starving. They knew they were putting their lives at risk, but the advancement of the kingdom of God was—and still is—their priority. One of my drivers had bullet holes in his vehicle from going into the war zone. He told me they recently drew fire from Russian Separatist snipers while driving on a particular road. The only thing he could do was speed away as fast as possible and trust God. That day they all made it out alive, but it was definitely a close call.

Lives Are Transformed In Chaos

One Friday my hosts told me they were going to take me into the war zone the following day to minister. They would be driving on the same road where their car was shot at just a few days ago. I said it was okay and chose to put my life in God's hands. I remember thinking that night about the possible outcomes. When I talked to my wife earlier that day, I didn't mention where I would be going the next morning. I didn't want her worrying about me. The next day they picked me up and we proceeded to the war zone. About two hours into our drive, two heavily-armed Russian helicopters approached us from the sky. They came within a couple hundred yards from us, and after a few moments, continued on their way. It was another chilling reminder for me that it was real. People died here. I could die here. I would have to find peace by trusting in the mighty God we serve and continue onward.

At one point along our journey, the driver suddenly floored the gas pedal, and we were soon racing at over 100 mph. The driver told me that this five-mile stretch of road is where the snipers had only days before shot at his car. On this day, though, no guns fired at us and for that we were thankful. The whole situation was surreal. While all of this took place, I remember laughing and thinking to myself, *How did I end up here?* We passed eight military road blocks on the way into the desolate city. By the time we arrived, I realized I was not just in the war zone, but I was on the front lines. Just across the field from where we stood were Russian Separatist soldiers.

All around us I saw destruction—buildings and homes in shattered ruins and roads that had been destroyed. Tanks and large artillery guns surrounded us. *Why*, I wondered, *are people still here? Why don't they leave the area?* The reason, I learned later, is that only those who have the financial means are able to escape the chaos in the cities. Others can escape if they have someplace they can go—perhaps a relative's home somewhere else in the nation. Unfortunately, about thirty percent of this city was unable to leave. They were prisoners in their own land.

Going in, I knew we couldn't stay long. We had to get in and get out. We were there to share the gospel and give the people bread and other basic goods. When we pulled into the meeting area, I was shocked to see hundreds of people waiting patiently for our arrival. We did not meet in a building but outside in the open. Military vehicles were all around us. We were informed that Ukrainian snipers were on top of some of the big buildings scouting out the enemy. This was the environment they brought me into to preach.

When it was time to introduce me, one from our group got up and simply announced, "This man has a message for you." Up to that point, I really didn't know what to say, but the Holy Spirit knew. As the war-weary, broken people gathered around, I looked into their eyes and saw profound hopelessness. The sorrow their eyes conveyed was heartbreaking. I knew that in an hour I would be leaving, and these people would not. I was standing dead center in their chaos, darkness, and confusion. Yet I know that we serve a God who is in that chaos. The Holy Spirit gave me an encouraging message of hope and salvation to deliver to the people. And that day, in the middle of a war-torn city, hundreds of people came to Christ.

After I finished speaking, I had a little time left before we had to head back out. I took this time to talk to the people there—old and young. Many shared sad stories of suffering and the deaths of loved ones. Students told me stories of bombs exploding in the school yards and how, when the sirens went off, the children panicked with anxiety. Young adults told me how many of their own friends had been killed. They all spoke of a great lack of food and water. It was truly heartbreaking.

Many things happened that day that will greatly impact my life forever. Yet one thing stands out the most. While I was preaching, one of the pastors' wives with us was standing next to a soldier. The soldier, perplexed as to why my friends kept coming to this war-torn city, asked her, "Why do you all keep coming here? Why do you risk your lives to come to this place?"

My friend's response was so real, so human, yet so powerful. She replied, "Honestly, I don't like coming here. I have a husband and kids and I know it is not safe to be here, but Jesus wants to be here, so we come."

God's People Are Willing To Enter Chaos

"Jesus wants to be here!" WOW! God's people are like fire beetles. When everyone else is running away from the chaos, God's people run to it. They want to see Jesus manifest in the madness. They are willing to risk everything for love's sake. They reap joy bringing Jesus to the chaos. Because of their love and sacrifice, thousands have been won to the Lord. Just as fire beetles are drawn to the mayhem of a forest fire to multiply, Christians are drawn to the mayhem of a war-torn region to reach the destitute for Christ.

The world around us is hurting. People everywhere are desperate for hope and a real sense of peace. Jesus came into this world to heal our brokenness and to set us free. He came into a broken, chaotic world being held captive by the enemy of our souls:

The Spirit of the Lord is upon Me, because He has anointed Me to preach the gospel to the poor; He has sent Me to heal the brokenhearted, to proclaim liberty to the captives and recovery of sight to the blind, to set at liberty those who are oppressed.

Luke 4:18 NKJV

Only Jesus can set the captive free. Only in Him can true life change begin. When we look around and see those who are hurting and broken, we should remember these words: "Jesus wants to be here!" Right in the mayhem, misery, hardship, troubles—in the chaos, wherever it may be.

Like fire beetles and the spirit-filled early church, let's be willing to go to the difficult places where the gospel message of salvation, hope, and freedom through Christ is needed most. Let's be willing to bring Jesus into their chaos.

CHAPTER 19

Stepping into Another's Chaos

"Then Peter said, 'Silver or gold I do not have, but what I do have I give you. In the name of Jesus Christ of Nazareth, walk.' Taking him by the right hand, he helped him up, and instantly the man's feet and ankles became strong. He jumped to his feet and began to walk. Then he went with them into the temple courts, walking and jumping, and praising God. When all the people saw him walking and praising God, they recognized him as the same man who used to sit begging at the temple gate called Beautiful, and they were filled with wonder and amazement at what had happened to him."

ACTS 3:6-10 NIV

God Is In Chaos Establishing His Will

It is amazing how God uses some seemingly, insignificant encounter in our lives to bring a mighty blessing to another person and great glory to His name.

Peter and John were simply going about their normal day's activities when a lame man asked them for money. Surely, it wasn't the first time a beggar had asked them for something. Peter didn't have any money to give, but, being filled with the Holy Spirit, he had something better –power in the name of Jesus. Peter commanded the lame man to walk and by faith he responded to Peter's word and walked. Clearly, this was a divine appointment orchestrated by the Holy Spirit.

I was at the end of another overseas ministry trip. On Saturday, I was informed that I would not be ministering at any church on Sunday. Instead, they wanted me to minister to an individual in great need of healing and deliverance. This person was a relative of one of the main church leaders. That was fine with me. That night, I packed my bags for the trip home after we met and attended to this individual's needs. I was very pleased at what the Lord accomplished on this trip. He confirmed His word with signs and wonders in every church we visited.

The next morning, they picked me up around 8:00 a.m. and we arrived forty-five minutes later. We met and prayed with the intended individual, who then received a powerful healing and deliverance. When we had concluded our work, someone came into the room and told me that I was now scheduled to preach somewhere that morning in another city. By this time, it was already 10:00 a.m. The service had already started, and we had an hour drive ahead of us. We had to hurry. I would be taken to the platform to preach as soon as we got there. In a split second, I went from feeling relaxed to a feeling of "Oh my!"

We rushed to the car and my driver sped away. I had never been to the city or the church where they were taking me. I knew nothing about it or even how this last-minute decision happened. I laughed inside as I contemplated how one goes from not speaking to speaking in the blink of an eye. I just smiled and asked the Lord to give me something to share.

Miracles Happen In Chaos

We arrived about an hour after the service had started. We walked into a church filled with a few hundred people. I was escorted up front and, within a couple of minutes, they gave me the microphone to preach. The Lord provided me a message to preach, and after the message I invited people to come forward for ministry. Many came forward seeking a touch from God. The Holy Spirit moved in power as I prayed for the needs of the people. The brokenhearted were healed and captives delivered from the grips of demons.

After I had finished praying for the last person, some people approached me and asked if I would pray for a friend. I agreed and enquired about their friend's need. They pointed to the other side of the church where he was sitting. They explained that he was crippled and could not walk. They had to carry him to the church that day and, in fact, had to carry him everywhere they went. In addition, he had to wear a diaper because of his condition.

I walked over to this pitiful-looking young man. He appeared to be in his early twenties. He waited patiently in a chair for his friends to come and get him. His face was downcast and his eyes void of hope. His legs and feet were twisted and

121

one of his arms was as well. We talked for a bit, and then I asked him if I could pray for him. In a weak voice, he answered, "Yes." I prayed a simple prayer of faith and healing over him. Then I reached down and grabbed his crippled, skinny, and twisted legs. One leg was more twisted than the other, but both of his feet were turned inward. I commanded his body to work and be healed in the name of Jesus. I looked deep into his eyes and said, "Stand up!"

By this time, everyone still in the church was watching with curiosity. People gasped as he found the courage to attempt standing up. He made it to his feet and then grabbed me as he began to fall. Standing there, I commanded him to walk. I kept telling him to walk. Slowly, he put one leg out as best as he could. I let go of him, and he very awkwardly started to walk. As he walked, his legs began to straighten. People watching were amazed by what they saw. The man that had to be carried everywhere was walking! The Lord completely healed the man. Every condition and ailment he had no longer existed and he no longer needed to wear diapers. His friends were free of carrying him everywhere and no longer needed to look after him anymore.

A few months later I had the opportunity to go back to the same church. While I was sitting in the front row, the pastor asked this young man to come to the front. I recall the expression he wore as he walked down the center aisle. His face was glowing with joy. He showed no signs of his previous conditions. The pastor asked him to share his testimony of God's wonderful grace and power.

When I think about this story, I am amazed at how God orchestrated it. I was not supposed to be there that day. I was not scheduled to preach anywhere. By the time I was informed that I would be preaching, the service had already begun. Understand this: God is always in the chaos, be it big or small, working out His perfect will. We just need to be ready to step into the chaos with Him and allow Him to use us as He sees fit.

CHAPTER 20

Inconvenient Surrender

"Many are the plans in a person's heart,
but it is the Lord's purpose that prevails."

PROVERBS 19:21 NIV

God's Will Is Not Always Convenient

In my travels, I have had some interesting personal experiences. To me, they appeared to be chaos, but after the fact, I saw the hand of God.

Once, as I was ministering overseas, it was about 10 p.m. on a Saturday night, and I was scheduled to preach at an influential bishop's church the next morning. I had ministered at this church on previous trips and earlier that week. The congregation knew I was scheduled to be there as it had been planned and advertised for some time. I looked forward to being there because many people had stories of miraculous healings and deliverances from our previous services. They wanted to share their stories with me before I left. I was delighted that I was finishing my trip at this church. I enjoyed being with the people there. As a bonus, the church was very close to the airport.

After the service, I would pack my bags and then head to the airport to begin the long journey home. As I was getting ready for the next morning's service, there was a knock on my door. I opened the door and saw my interpreter standing there. She told me she just received a call saying there has been a change of plans regarding the morning. She informed me that I would not be speaking at the bishop's church. Instead, someone would pick us up and drive us to another city a few hours away to minister there.

Honestly, when I heard that news, I was upset. I had been extremely busy ministering in this region of the world for some time. I was looking forward to concluding my trip at the church I was scheduled to be in before going home to be with my family. In addition, it would only take me five minutes to get to the church. The airport was also just minutes away. Now, late at night, I learn that I'm not preaching in the church where I was scheduled. To make matters even worse, we had to drive several hours to another church...on horrible roads! Then we had to hurry back and hope I don't miss my flight. I thought this was a crazy idea.

Faith Looks Beyond The Chaos And Finds God

Given the situation, I came very close to saying "No!" to this change of plan. I was thinking that I should just forget it and stay in the city and not feel rushed about catching my flight. I was also upset that the church leadership would spring this on me on such short notice. I looked at my interpreter, and she could tell I was not at all pleased with the new plan. Then, in my moment of pouting and frustration, the Lord spoke to me in a calm, still voice, saying, "Mike, there are people there that need Me." With those words, the Lord got my attention. My heart immediately changed, and I realized the Lord's hand was in this. This was not man's doing, but God's. This was not the first time—nor would it be the last—that I needed to look past the chaos and find God. I have learned that the Holy Spirit is good at making plans, and His plans are always good. I pulled myself together, looked at my interpreter, and told her what the Lord had said to me.

The morning came quickly, and we left very early so we would be sure to make it to the church on time. The drive was a lot longer than expected, so we were a little late for the service. We walked into a very small room filled with people. As we entered the room, the people stopped what they were doing and began to applaud our arrival. The joy on their faces to have a guest speaker from another country was humbling. I then realized that these people probably have never had a guest speaker from another country. It is, perhaps, a very rare occasion when anyone comes to them.

This little church was only six months old. The pastor had another church prior to this one, but he and his family had to flee because of persecution. They came into this city where it was safer to start a new church. Then, like a light going on in my head, I remembered how upset I felt about the inconvenience of my plans being changed! God is in the chaos! At the time, I did not see Him right away. But He was there, orchestrating His plan and purpose. There were people that needed Him desperately. They needed a miracle in their lives. They needed to experience the embrace of God's presence. And to think I could have—and almost did—miss out on the magnificence of God's divine will.

After a few songs, I was invited up to speak. There was no sound system and, to be sure, none was needed given the size of the room. There were about fifty people there altogether. Within this small group, the Lord had told me, there were people that needed Him, and He had prepared a special message just for them. About ten minutes into the message, my interpreter and I felt the glory of the Lord come into the room. His presence was very heavy and prevailing. A few minutes later, miracles began to take place. These oppressed people were being overwhelmed with the glory of the Lord. People started to experience mighty deliverances; demons manifested and were driven out.

One woman we prayed for went flying backward as a demon of witchcraft displayed itself and took over her body. I commanded the demon to leave in the name of Jesus. The demon departed her body, shrieking as it left. The woman came back to herself and quickly jumped to her feet. She started jumping up and down, rejoicing at her deliverance. She then paused, realizing something else had happened. She screamed, "I can see! I can see!" The Lord had supernaturally healed her. Her vision was completely restored. Other people in the church experienced healings and deliverances. It was an incredible service that God had put together.

Thinking back, I am amazed at how God intervened the previous night. There I was, thinking how awful and inconvenient this change of plans would be for me. The audacity of the church leadership to send me so far away the day I had to catch a flight home was agitating. But God's plan was different than my plan. There were other people that needed Him. God was teaching me that He is always there...in the chaos...in our confusion. When we get frustrated with our circumstances, we need to pause and seek Him. He is there, waiting, because there are people that need Him.

God's will is not just about us. It's about His kingdom. We are called to be His hands and feet. Sometimes we miss God's will because we get caught up in our own desires and not His. I wonder how many times in my life I have missed out on God's will because all I could see was me and what I wanted. I'm humbled when I think of all the people who would not have received their miraculous deliverances and healings that day simply because I was angry my plans had changed. I had wanted to spend my last day giving a quick sermon, getting on a jet, and looking back on all the wonderful things God had done earlier in the trip. It wasn't meant to be. God was going to push me forward because He hadn't finished performing His wonders on this trip.

Good Things Happen When We Surrender

If we really want to pursue His kingdom, we must accept the fact that things will not always go our way. There will be times when there will be inconveniences to us. When we find ourselves getting upset over petty things, we must pause and listen. Perhaps God is getting ready to speak. Perhaps He has prepared another way that is even better. After all, there are other people that need Him in their lives and in their circumstances. Perhaps God is getting ready to do the miraculous through you.

CHAPTER 21

Stand Your Ground

"Therefore, take up the whole armor of God,
that you may be able to withstand in the evil day,
and having done all, to stand."

EPHESIANS 6:13 NKJV

We Are God's Hands And Feet In The Chaos

Chaotic situations often produce fear. Fear is a tool the devil uses to hinder us from finding God in our dire situations. I have found myself in many situations that necessitated my transitioning from fear to faith quickly. Without this transition, the forces of darkness can be victorious in the chaos. Believe me, evil spirits know whether you have real faith. You can be a Christian whose faith is weakened because of the circumstances of a strenuous situation facing you. It is at such times the enemy presses you to find out if you truly believe you have power over him. He will press hard, pushing back with fear. When you learn to find God in chaos, you can begin to develop mountain-moving faith. When you can transition your fears to faith, demonic forces must back down.

On many occasions, demons have used fear to try to get me to back down. Very often during a deliverance, a demon would manifest and speak through the individual. It would say things to intimidate me into stopping. Once I was preaching in Eastern Ukraine, mostly a Russian speaking area. One evening, while providing ministry to an individual, a demon came forth and began to threaten me. When this happens, the demon will usually speak in the person's native language, and my interpreter translates the interchange. In this case, it came up speaking Russian, the only language the man knew.

This evil spirit continuously hurled threats at me in Russian, and my interpreter translated what it was saying. The demon's strategy wasn't working. I had seen this happen many times in the past; they are just powerless threats. After a few minutes of this, the demon slowly moved directly in front of my face. Then it tried a new tactic: it spoke to me in perfect English. "You are nothing but a weak American, and I will destroy you!" it sneered. At this, I looked at my interpreter and said, sarcastically, "You do not need to interpret that for me." We both laughed as we knew through Christ we had the victory over this demon.

The evil spirit knew it was defeated because we were not cowering in fear. I drove the demon out of the man and he was set free through the power of Jesus Christ.

The Authority Of The Believer Is Victorious In Chaos

One of the most confrontational deliverances I ever conducted involved a prominent leader in the occult. My phone rang and the voice on the other end sounded calm but desperate. The man told me he was passing through town, and he was in a hotel room. He introduced himself as Kevin and said he was a warlock in this particular occultist group. He gave me the priestly name by which the occult world knew him and told me to look him up on the internet. He shared his story and asked me if I could help him. He wanted to get out of the occult and turn his life over to Jesus. He asked me if Jesus would still accept him, because he had done a lot of bad things. I assured him that it was possible.

Once I got off the phone with him I looked him up on the internet. He was not joking. He was exactly what he said he was. He was a full-fledged warlock. His situation was urgent, so I arranged to meet him. I called some friends and asked them to go with me. It was night, and we had to drive about sixty miles to where he was staying. We pulled into the parking lot around 10 p.m. The hotel was on a back road a few miles from the interstate and looked like something out of a horror movie.

Our Faith Is Challenged In The Darkness

My friends began to get a little nervous. We wondered if we were being led into an ambush by people from the occult. We proceeded by faith, trusting in the power of Christ over the forces of evil. We knew we were walking into a very chaotic situation. We got to the door and knocked. Kevin reluctantly opened the door but ignored us for a moment. I looked at him and asked if it was alright to come in. He gave no response. I recognized the countenance on his face as one that I had seen many times in the past. It was an expression of evil.

Kevin sat on the bed and continued to ignore us. We noticed he was fixated on the television; it seemed odd. We turned to look at the television and realized he was watching a satanic program. The program showed a man wearing a goat's head and ranting hateful things. I then realized what was happening. The demon inside of Kevin had taken over him. The devil was not willing to let him go free.

I looked at one of my friends and told him to turn the television off. When my friend picked up the remote, the demon growled, "Don't you touch that!" Once again, I told my friend, "Turn it off!" When the TV went silent the demon stood up in a rage and said, "Leave now!" And the television turned back on. "No, we will not leave!" I countered.

I knew Kevin wanted us there. I confirmed that with him before we arrived. His will had reached out to me asking for help when he made that phone call. I turned the television off again. The demon turned it back on and tried to ignore us. I turned it off again. The demon then turned to me and began to threaten all of us, telling us to leave before he destroyed us. I ordered the evil spirit to let me speak to Kevin. I commanded it to go down in the name of Jesus and for Kevin to come up. In a moment's time, the shift took place. Kevin was back to himself. He was in a daze, wondering what was happening and how we got in. I quickly explained to him, as best as I could, what had taken place. Given the situation, I knew I had to move quickly. I had Kevin confirm he wanted our help. I led him in a sinner's prayer to receive Jesus as his Lord and Savior. Doing so allowed God to immediately come into Kevin's chaos and enabled us to minister in this chaos. This was the very thing the demon feared would happen and the reason it tried to get us to leave before we even began. The enemy knows the power of Christ, but it also knows the weakness of man. Consequently, the devil does not give up so easily.

Once we had confirmed Kevin wanted us there and established his faith in Christ, I commanded the demon to come back up. Suddenly, evil and hate appeared in its eyes again. The demon was back. It looked at us and told us to leave or it would destroy us. I looked back into its eyes and said, "No, Kevin wants us here and you must go!" The demon persisted with more threats. At one point, it looked at me and said, "Who do you think you are! You are not even Magi! I told you, boy, leave before I kill you!" I refused, and the demon didn't like it. The enraged spirit raised its voice at me and said, "Leave now before it's too late! You are running out of time!"

Suddenly, the lights went out in the room. The demon had supernaturally turned them off. My friends and I now stood in the darkness with an infuriated demon speaking through Kevin.

Faith Takes Its Stand In The Darkness

In the darkness, you could feel the fear creeping into the room as the threats kept coming: "See? I told you, you had better leave before I destroy all of you!"

The enemy will push you to the edge to see whether you truly believe. It was at this point one of the men in our group wanted to leave as quickly as possible. But it is in this type of chaos that you must find the strength to stand. And you must stand in faith. You must believe that God is with you in the chaos:

> Therefore, put on the complete armor of God, so that you will be able to [successfully] resist and stand your ground in the evil day [of danger], and having done everything [that the crisis demands], to stand firm [in your place, fully prepared, immovable, victorious].

Ephesians 6:13 AMP

When we are face-to-face with our evil adversary, we are called to stand our ground. Even if the situation is completely out of control, even though it feels as if all hell is coming against us, we are called to stand!

At this moment, we had two choices. We could run out the door and allow fear to overcome us or we could stand our ground. I made the decision to stand on the word of God and call the devil's bluff. We refused to budge. I looked right back at the demon and declared that I had authority over it in Jesus's name. The demon moved closer to me in the darkness and said, "Watch me turn them back on!" Instantly, the lights supernaturally came back on. The devil attempted to instill fear in us by demonstrating its power with the lights. And, yes, demons have powers. They realize they are defeated through the authority of Jesus Christ, but they also know that you must believe it. Your faith must be real. When we activate true faith in the time of chaos, God moves. He is always there, but we must find Him by faith. When we find Him, He will manifest His glory.

When the lights turned back on, the devil looked at me. It was a different look; it knew its time was up. I took command over the demon spirit in Kevin. Quickly, the boldness it had been exhibiting began to evaporate. It knew that we understood we had all power over it. When the demon saw our faith was genuine, it backed down. Under the authority of the living Son of God, we drove the demon out from Kevin.

Sometimes deliverance happens quickly. Sometimes it can be a real battle. Yet through Christ, we always win. The Lord is always there; we must learn to find Him. Even the devil knows God is present in these battles. Yet, for whatever reason, God wants us to be His hands and His feet in the chaos.

He chooses to use us to do His mighty works. When we operate in true faith, we will see God's greatness manifested. He told us to go and preach the gospel to the world and promised us He would never leave nor forsake us. He is always with us... in every situation...so STAND!

CHAPTER 22

Finding God in Ziklag

*"But David encouraged himself
in the Lord his God."*

I SAMUEL 30:6 KJV

God Delights In Helping His Children

Chaos happens in all our lives. It comes upon believers and
non-believers alike. The difference is that believers know who
to turn to in their time of trouble. They know who to trust in
their trouble. Non-believers also can turn to the Lord for help
when they choose to surrender their lives to Him. He wants to
help all who call upon His name.

David and his men returned home to Ziklag. Their hearts
fainted with the terror they beheld. Their homes had been
plundered and totally destroyed. Everything had been burnt
to the ground. Like that wasn't bad enough. Their enemy, the
Amalekites, also had taken their families captive. Overtaken
by fear of the unknown, of their families' condition, they wept
bitterly until they could weep no more. Suddenly, the men

turn their attention to David and anger built up in their hearts toward him. In their distress, they talked about stoning him.

David suddenly found himself in great danger at the hands of his own men. At this point, David could have chosen to run. He could have picked up weapons in preparation for a fight. He simply could have lain down and given up. After all, even his own family was captured. David did none of these. In this chaotic situation, David turned his attention to the Lord. Scripture says, "But David encouraged himself in the Lord his God" (KJV). In David's time of great need, he needed strength to continue. He needed to find a way out of this dark place of torment. He turned his attention to the Lord. He chose to find God in the chaos.

This wasn't the first time David found strength in a difficult time. He had learned as a youth to trust in the Lord God of Israel. While he tended his father's sheep, a lion and a bear attacked, but the Lord delivered him. When Goliath taunted Israel, David took his stand by faith and defeated the giant. He had developed a pattern of turning to God in his time of need. He had learned time and time again that the Lord could and would rescue him whenever he cried out for help. David had the revelation that God indeed was present. God would be there in his time of need. Ziklag was no different.

The Lord's Purpose Prevails

Yes, what had happened was horrific, yet David did not give in to the circumstances that surrounded him. He knew once again who to turn to for help. Not only did he know who to look for, he knew how to find Him. And he did! David's first response was to encourage himself in the Lord his God. Then he turned to the Lord to help guide him in this situation. God assured David that He would be victorious in battle and would also rescue everyone that had been taken captive.

Encouraged by faith, David was able to rally his men and go after the enemy. Just like God had promised, they defeated the enemy and got back everything that was taken.

Like David, when we find ourselves at our faith's most vulnerable moments, we need to find God. We need to seek Him for He is near. He is right beside us waiting for us to cry out in our time of need. When we do this, our faith will be strengthened, and our victory is sure. God is always with us waiting patiently on us to turn to Him. He delights in helping His children.

May we quickly learn that God is in our confusion, He is in our struggle, and He is in our chaos. He waits patiently on us to find Him and He longs to help us in our time of need.

The Final Chapter

*"Jesus came up and said to them, "All authority
(all power of absolute rule) in heaven and on earth
has been given to Me. Go therefore and make
disciples of all the nations [help the people to learn
of Me, believe in Me, and obey My words],
baptizing them in the name of the Father and
of the Son and of the Holy Spirit, teaching them
to observe everything that I have commanded you;
and lo, I am with you always [remaining with you
perpetually—regardless of circumstance, and on
every occasion], even to the end of the age."*

MATTHEW 28:18-20 AMP

Chaos happens. You can't sidestep it. Chaotic events can be
brief or go on for long periods of time. They can be extreme—a
loved one's death, medical emergencies, dangerous situations—
or just plain, everyday occurrences that momentarily turn our
world upside down, like an inconvenient or stressful incident.
Whatever kind of confusion, disorder, or madness you are
facing, you can cry out to your Heavenly Father for help.

God Is With You In The Chaos

No matter what chaotic situation you are experiencing, God knows what you are facing. He is omnipresent! He stands right beside you in your chaos, waiting for you to exercise your faith in His ability and for you to cry out to Him in your time of need. He delights in helping His children.

What will you do the next time you find yourself engulfed by chaos? Face it alone? No! Rather, seek God—and find Him—for He is near. When you do, your faith will be strengthened, and your victory will be sure...for God is in the chaos!

For more information about *Free the Nations* go to:

www.freethenations.org